AS/A-LEVEL

Film Studies

Tanya Jones

ESSENTIAL WORD
DICTIONARY

D0228205

Philip Allan Updates
Market Place
Deddington
Oxfordshire
OX15 0SE

Tel: 01869 338652
Fax: 01869 337590
e-mail: sales@philipallan.co.uk
www.philipallan.co.uk

ISBN 0 86003 383 X

Printed by Raithby, Lawrence & Co Ltd, Leicester

P00223

Introduction

This *Essential Word Dictionary* aims to provide you with invaluable definitions for AS and A2 film studies. Your film studies course will require you to discuss the technical, textual and institutional aspects of film and the definitions in this dictionary cover all of these areas. Whether you are studying the processes of film production, the textual elements within a particular film, the key personnel who create a film, the audiences who consume films or the organisations/companies behind film-making, the terms you need to know are listed in these pages.

For each of the terms in this dictionary, an initial definition is given followed by an extension of that definition. There are also examples which will help to illustrate the meaning of the term. In many cases tips are included on applications of the term or issues you should be aware of in association with it. Throughout the dictionary there are cross-references to words and phrases defined elsewhere which are shown in this *italic* font.

Any essay or study which you write during your course will need to include specific film terms, used accurately and appropriately. Read the definitions in this dictionary carefully and check the examples given in order to make sure that the term is appropriate to the subject which you are analysing. One good test of this is to substitute your example for the ones listed in the definition and check that it fits the context.

This dictionary has been written to fulfil the criteria of AS and A2 film studies. It only contains terms which you might come across in the course of your studies at this level. Other film studies dictionaries are available, but many are aimed at an undergraduate market and therefore contain terms which you will not need. Use this dictionary to check your knowledge of terminology and to ensure that your essays are accurate and comprehensive.

above-the-line costs: the costs of a film before shooting begins.

■ These costs include those for locations, screen writers, directors and actors. Above-the-line costs tend to be less than those incurred after the shooting of the film has finished, such as marketing costs.

■ *TIP* The balance of above-the-line to *below-the-line costs* has shifted over the last 20 years and today a film's above-the-line costs might only constitute 50% of its entire budget.

abstract film: a style of film which communicates its meaning through the use of colours, lines and objects.

■ Abstract films do not use *narratives* and have no real connection to reality. The meanings within these films are interpreted through random and unconnected visuals.

■ *e.g.* Man Ray's 1920s' film, *L' Etoile de mer*

Academy Awards (also known as the *Oscars*): annual awards presented by the *Academy of Motion Pictures Arts and Sciences* to performers and technicians in the film industry.

Academy of Motion Pictures Arts and Sciences: an honorary organisation comprising actors and technicians in the film industry, founded in 1927 to promote film.

■ The academy is responsible for nominating and choosing the winners for the *Academy Awards*.

accelerated montage: a type of *editing* in which different images are seen to move from one to the other incredibly rapidly.

■ Accelerated montage is often used in sequences to generate a sense of frantic or frenetic action. Many different *cuts* are used within a very short space of time, often in order to imply the chaotic nature of an event.

■ *e.g.* The 'shower scene' from Hitchcock's *Psycho* (1960) includes a sequence of extremely quick cuts from the knife to the increasingly bloody body of

Marion Crane. The technique of accelerated montage is used here to reflect the horror of the event and the frantic nature of the killing.

action film: a film which includes a fast-paced storyline (often highly *choreographed*), physical action sequences, elaborate stunts and *pyrotechnic* displays. The action is more important than the dialogue in this type of film.
- Action films make up a large percentage of *Hollywood*'s film output. They may be expensive to produce, but if marketed correctly, e.g. as the summer *blockbuster*, and with the right actor in the lead role, they can make enormous profits for the film producers.
- *e.g.* *Speed* (Jan de Bont, 1994), *The Long Kiss Goodnight* (Renny Harlin, 1996)

action still: a photograph which has been blown up from the negative of a film.
- Action stills are different from *publicity stills*, which are shot during production with a still camera.

actor: an individual who plays a part in a film.
- It is possible to differentiate between *stars* (those actors who are seen as good *box office* bets by film producers) and other actors.

Actor's Studio: founded in 1947 by Elia Kazan, in New York.
- Most famous for the teaching of *method acting*, which aims to create a natural performance, the Actor's Studio taught that in order to generate a *character* effectively, the actor had to enter into the psychology of that character. Creating the emotional history of the character was as important as creating an appropriate physical appearance.

adventure film: a film in which the main characters are placed in an environment which is not their normal one and are faced with danger and/or excitement.
- Adventure films often include a storyline in which a character faces a number of challenges in order to achieve a goal. These challenges are usually physical, as well as psychological and emotional. There is some overlap between *action films* and adventure films, but adventure films often have much more exotic or unusual locations.
- *e.g.* *Steven Spielberg*'s *Indiana Jones* trilogy

aerial shot: a camera shot taken from an overhead position, as if from a bird's-eye view. The camera is often mounted on an aeroplane or a helicopter.
- Aerial shots are frequently used at the beginning of films to introduce the *location* of the story. See also *establishing shot*.
- *e.g.* The opening sequence to Anthony Minghella's *The English Patient* (1996) begins with a stunning aerial shot of the desert in order to introduce the audience to a location which is significant within the film.

agent: a person who acts on behalf of a client, in this case an actor, a director or another member of a film crew.

■ Agents negotiate the terms of their clients' contracts, including how much they are paid, what conditions they work in and what extras can be demanded. Agents take a percentage of the actor's or director's fee for their services.

Almodóvar, Pedro (1951–): film director.

■ Born in Calzada de Calatrava in La Mancha in Spain, Almodóvar began making amateur films at an early age. However, it was not until the death of Franco in 1975 and the subsequent artistic explosion that he was able to produce and direct films for release in the cinema. Almodóvar was one of a group of artists working in Madrid in the late 1970s who were part of La Movida, an artistic and cultural movement which celebrated the freedom that came after Franco's death by creating exuberant and entirely liberal art. He is often credited with changing the way in which other countries view Spain, by creating an image of a modern, dynamic country.

■ Filmography: *Pepi, Luci, Bom and Other Girls on the Heap* (1980), *Labyrinth of Passion* (1982), *Dark Habits* (1983), *What Have I Done to Deserve This?* (1984), *Law of Desire* (1987), *Matador* (1988), *Women on the Verge of a Nervous Breakdown* (1988), *Tie Me Up! Tie Me Down!* (1989), *High Heels* (1991), *Kika* (1993), *The Flower of My Secret* (1995), *Live Flesh* (1997), *All About My Mother* (1999), *Talk to Her* (2002)

ambient sound: the normal sound which exists in a particular scene or location.

■ *e.g.* traffic noise, bird song and crowd chatter

■ *TIP* Ambient sound can exist in any location. To describe sound which exists only in the fictional story of a film, see *diegetic sound*.

American Dream: the belief that anyone in America, regardless of their background, can achieve their dreams.

■ The idea of the American Dream was popularised in writing concerning the American Goldrush and has become a central part of the US publicity machine. Individuals who struck a main source of gold could find themselves immediately wealthy. The fact that, given the right financial backing and the right policies, anyone can become president of the United States contributes to the notion that anyone can achieve anything in America. Films concerned with the American Dream often have storylines which see the 'little man' triumphing against adversity.

■ There are probably more contemporary films which satirise the American Dream than those which promote it.

■ *e.g.* *Forrest Gump* (Robert Zemeckis, 1994) tells the story of an individual who overcame considerable personal problems to achieve success.

a

analogue: a technology for the recording and transmission of sound and images.

■ Analogue processes are currently being overtaken by digital recording and transmission processes.

animation: the process by which inanimate objects are made to appear to move.

■ Traditionally, this has been achieved by shooting a series of drawings which have fractional variations and then running the series together to create a sense of movement. *Stop-motion animation* is achieved by slightly altering the position of a model before each shot is taken. Nowadays animation is mostly done using *computer-generated imagery* rather than by hand.

■ *e.g.* *King Kong* (Ernest B. Schoedask, 1933), *Disney*'s *Snow White and the Seven Dwarfs* (1937)

animator: an artist who does the drawings for an *animation*.

aperture: the opening in a *lens* or a *camera* which controls the amount of light the film is exposed to.

■ The extent to which the aperture of the camera is opened determines not only how much light is eventually seen within the shot, but also how much of the image is filmed. If the director only wishes to film a small section of the image, the aperture will be very small.

archetype: a basic character type which has appeared in many films and has become recognisable to the viewer.

■ Archetypes can range from the doomed lover to the character who sells his soul to the devil.

■ *e.g.* Baz Luhrmann's *William Shakespeare's Romeo + Juliet* uses the doomed lover archetype.

archive: a collection of films and documents concerning film.

■ Archives are a means of preserving films which are no longer in current circulation.

■ *e.g.* The British Film Institute (BFI) has an extensive film archive.

Art Cinema: a certain type of cinema which is experimental in technique and narrative.

■ The term 'Art Cinema' is often used to describe films which are unusual stylistically and are not aimed at a *mainstream cinema* audience. The directors of these films usually exercise a high degree of control over the film-making process.

■ *e.g.* the films of *French New Wave* directors Godard and Cocteau

■ *TIP* The term 'Art Cinema' is one which excites much debate, especially in connection with *censorship* and classification. Traditionally, audiences of Art Cinema are deemed to be more discerning and better educated than mainstream audiences and thus more able to understand complex themes and to contend with controversial or explicit subject matter. Art Cinema products have been treated less severely by the *British Board of Film Classification* because of this, but many critics argue that this sets up a problematic hierarchy of audiences, with unfair or inaccurate assumptions about individual audience members' responses.

artificial light: a source of light other than sunlight, moonlight or firelight, which is created by lighting equipment. See also *available light*.

assistant director: a member of the film crew who works closely with the *director*.
■ The assistant director (AD) is responsible for the smooth daily running of the shoot. He/she is responsible for scheduling the shooting days, dealing with *extras* and organising *call sheets* for the *cast* and *crew*.

asynchronous sound: an effect which occurs when the sound is either intentionally or unintentionally out of sync with the image.
■ If the sound is unintentionally asynchronous, this is the product of bad editing. If intentionally asynchronous, the film-maker is usually attempting to indicate to the viewers that they are watching something unreal and not observing real life.

audience: the individuals or group who watch a film.
■ Films are produced for an audience; they are products which are sold to consumers. The film industry uses countless strategies to encourage consumers to spend their 'leisure pound' (the money reserved for entertainment) at the cinema, such as complex publicity campaigns and merchandising.
■ Studies of audiences usually focus on differences in age, gender and cultural background, as well as on the ways in which an audience might consume or interpret films.
■ *TIP* In order to discuss questions of audience fully, consider who watches films, how, why and where. Remember that *producers* and audiences are interlinked and affect each other. Both are 'active' within the film industry and within film consumption. Film companies may try to construct a potential market for their films through advertising campaigns, but audience members can also affect the industry by reviewing films on the internet, spreading opinion via good or bad word of mouth or opting not to see certain types of films which they consider to be no longer fashionable.

audio: relates to any part of a film which can be heard, rather than seen.

auteur: a French word meaning author, used to refer to a *director* with a distinctive personal style.

■ The term is usually attached to directors who have exhibited signature characteristics across a range of their films. Such characteristics may include repeated use of specific camera movement, an exploration of particular themes or the regular use of narrative elements.

■ *e.g.* Alfred Hitchcock is renowned for his particular use of the *thriller* genre, involving flawed male protagonists and aloof, blonde, female characters.

■ *TIP* It is worth noting that some critics argue that creating a distinction between auteurs and other directors establishes an elitism within the film industry.

auteur theory: discusses whether a *director* can be given the title *auteur*.

■ Auteur theory considers whether a director shows a consistency of style or theme which makes his/her films recognisable to the viewer.

■ *TIP* Auteur theory is much debated and some critics argue that it is an artificial means by which some directors can be given more status than others.

available light: any type of natural light, such as sunlight, moonlight and firelight, which can be used during the shooting of scenes. See also *artificial light*.

B-movies: a term used to describe cheap and quickly made films.

■ B-movies first came to prominence in the United States during the Depression of the 1930s. Audiences wanted an experience which gave them value for money, and cheap films could be shown as *double bills* while still allowing the cinema to make money.

back lighting: a term used to describe the light source which comes from behind a character.

■ If the only lighting in a scene is back lighting, silhouettes can be created. Back lighting can be used to create mystery around a character and tension in the audience.

back lot: the area within a film studio complex which has been designated as the place where exterior shots will be filmed.

back projection: a filming technique in which live action is filmed in front of a screen onto which the background action is projected.

■ This technique was prevalent from the 1920s to the 1980s and was often used in scenes in which characters were 'driving'. The road and any buildings the characters were passing were back projected onto a screen and the actors were filmed sitting in a stationary car in front of the screen. The effect generated was designed to approximate the real action of characters moving within a car, without the problems of having to mount a camera on a truck in front of a moving vehicle and film the actors while they were really driving.

back story: the information in a script which gives extra details about characters.

■ Back story is a *screen writer's* term for the detail about characters included to make them seem more believable and realistic.

■ *e.g.* Information about a character's past will be included in order to help the viewer understand the character's actions and motivations.

■ *TIP* Mainstream big-budget films usually include a back story so as to be comprehensible to the widest possible audience. Independent and art-house films do not always include this information, thus retaining a sense of mystery about characters.

BAFTA: see *British Academy of Film and Television Arts.*

BBFC: see *British Board of Film Classification.*

behind-the-scenes footage: filmed material showing the making of a film.

■ Behind-the-scenes footage often shows actors' preparations, the organisation and set-up of particular scenes and the processes behind *special effects*. This kind of footage is often included within *DVD* versions of a film and is designed to give the viewer information about production processes.

■ *e.g.* *Heart of Darkness: A Filmmaker's Apocalypse* (1991) provided an account of the troubled filming of *Francis Ford Coppola*'s film *Apocalypse Now* (1979).

below-the-line costs: the costs of a film after shooting has begun.

■ Below-the-line costs include *editing* and *marketing*. These costs can be enormous for a film production company, as trailer and poster campaigns etc. can prove very expensive. The big studios and film companies can afford far more, in terms of below-the-line costs, than their smaller counterparts. This gives the companies with the most money the greatest power to get their films known by potential audiences. See also *above-the-line costs.*

Bertolucci, Bernardo (1940–): film *director.*

■ Born in Palma, Italy, Bertolucci has made films in English and Italian. His most controversial film was *Last Tango in Paris* (1972), which was passed with an X certificate by the British Board of Film Classification in Britain but banned in Italy, where Bertolucci, the film's producer and its star (Marlon Brando) each received a 3-month suspended jail sentence.

■ Filmography: *The Grim Reaper* (1962), *Before the Revolution* (1964), *The Spider's Strategem* (1970), *The Conformist* (1970), *Last Tango in Paris* (1972), *The Tragedy of a Ridiculous Man* (1981), *The Last Emperor* (1987), *The Sheltering Sky* (1990), *Little Buddha* (1993), *Stealing Beauty* (1996), *Besieged* (1998)

Besson, Luc (1959–): film *director.*

■ Born in Paris, Besson first cherished an ambition to be a deep-sea diver, but after a diving accident in 1976 he could no longer pursue that career. His love of the sea and fascination with deep-sea diving was the impetus for his 1988 film *The Big Blue*. Besson owns several production companies (Films du Loup, Films du Dauphin and Leeloo Productions).

■ Filmography: *The Last Battle* (1983), *Subway* (1985), *The Big Blue* (1988), *Nikita* (1990), *Atlantis* (1991), *Leon* (1994), *The Fifth Element* (1997), *Joan of Arc* (1999)

Bigelow, Kathryn (1952–): film *director.*

■ Born in California, Kathryn Bigelow is one of the handful of female directors who are given big-budget *Hollywood* films to direct. She has also worked within *genres* that have traditionally been the territory of male directors, such as action (*Point Break,* 1991) and thriller (*Blue Steel,* 1990).

■ Filmography: *The Loveless* (1981), *Near Dark* (1987), *Blue Steel* (1990), *Point Break* (1991), *Strange Days* (1995), *The Weight of Water* (2000)

big-screen cinema: describes films shown on a much larger than normal screen.

■ The spectacle of viewing images on large screens is not a twentieth-century phenomenon. Audiences in the early nineteenth century had access to diorama productions, one of the most dramatic of which was *L'Arrivée d'un train en gare* filmed in 1896 by Louis Lumière. Large landscapes were painted onto a huge transparent canvas and the audience watched the image as variations in lighting projected through the canvas made it appear to move. Because of the size of the canvas, members of the audience had the sensation that they were being pulled into the image, thus taking part in the experience represented on screen. This form of early visual spectacle was an attempt to approximate reality by creating a complete viewing experience.

■ Cinema continued to experiment with wide-screen technologies, and with the advent of *sound* and *colour* what was offered became even more exciting for the audience. The next stages of development saw Fox projecting films in 70 mm Grandeur; Paramount's equivalent was Magnafilm and Warner Bros' format was VitaScope. None of these proved to be particularly successful, partly because of the advent of an alternative new viewing experience in the form of television. It was not until the 1950s when Cinerama was introduced that wide-screen technologies became popular with audiences again. Films in this format tended to be of real events, and in some cases the viewing experience was so realistic that members of the audience ran out of the cinema. CinemaScope was to be the next major advance for the big screen and was developed by Twentieth Century Fox to deliver an even more realistic and exciting film experience.

■ Today, it is not just the screen in this type of cinema which is bigger. Projectors, film stock, cameras and sound equipment are also significantly larger. Films using this technology are often experience-driven rather than narrative-driven.

■ *e.g.* **IMAX** cinemas use 70 mm film stock (rather than the standard 35 mm) and projectors the size of small cars. They show films which give the viewer an experience of being in space, under the water or on a roller coaster.

billing: describes the position and size of the actor's or director's name on publicity material such as film posters.

■ The position and size of an actor's or director's name on a poster is important. If the name is positioned first or at the top of a poster, that individual is said to have 'top billing' and therefore most status.

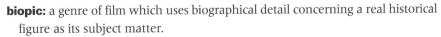

biopic: a genre of film which uses biographical detail concerning a real historical figure as its subject matter.

■ Biopics may embellish events in order to make the individuals concerned more attractive to cinema audiences.

■ *e.g. Iris* (Richard Eyre, 2001), a film which details the life of writer Iris Murdoch

Black Cinema: refers to African-American films made by black film-makers.

■ These films often concentrate on the experiences of African-Americans within the United States or another multiracial context.

■ *e.g.* the films of director *Spike Lee*, such as *Do The Right Thing* (1989)

blacklist: a list of names of film actors or crew members who have been discriminated against because of their political affiliations, gender, race, nationality or sexual orientation.

■ A blacklist is created when an organisation or individual wishes to discriminate against others.

■ *e.g.* Possibly the most famous example of a blacklist was that created in 1950s America at a time of paranoia about Communist invasion or infiltration. Senator Joseph R. McCarthy and his supporters created a list of any artist deemed to have Communist sympathies. People named on the list were then barred from creating films, having novels published etc.

blaxploitation films: a term used mainly to describe films made in America in the 1960s and 1970s, which featured black central characters and often sensational storylines.

■ Blaxploitation films were aimed at a black audience and thus constituted a significant departure from the standard cinema offerings which seemed to be targeted at a purely white audience.

■ *e.g. Shaft* (Gordon Parks, 1971)

blockbuster: a term used to describe big-budget *Hollywood* films.

■ Blockbusters are often characterised by big budgets, lots of action, universally recognisable characters and storylines, and special effects. Film studios rely on summer blockbusters to make enough of a *box-office* profit to compensate for losses incurred by less successful films. Blockbusters have been described as a genre in their own right, as they have a set of recognisable characteristics.

(1) The basic storyline of a film is simple and universally recognisable. In order for a film to succeed outside an English-speaking market, it must be based on a story type which has universal appeal. Many films make the majority of their profits from international sales, either at the box office or on VHS and DVD, and therefore need to be understood outside an American market.

(2) Characters are simple to understand. The characters in blockbusters do not have complicated psychological conditions or motivations. They are not stereotypes either, but individuals with whom the viewer can easily identify.

(3) The film is sold on its 'look'. Much of the cost of blockbusters and high-concept films goes on special effects and high production values (the film looks slick and expensive). Huge set pieces and dramatic new special effects are a perfect marketing focus for film producers. Viewers do not expect subtlety of characterisation or complexity of plot from a blockbuster, but they do expect a spectacular piece of entertainment.

(4) The film is only the beginning. The huge initial investment needed to produce blockbusters/high-concept films is not quite the gamble it might initially seem. Advertising budgets are extremely high and many films do not breakeven at the box office. However, with a film which has universal appeal, the potential profit from the sale of satellite and terrestrial television rights, VHS/DVD sales and merchandising is enormous.

■ *e.g.* *Terminator 2* (*James Cameron*, 1991), *Spiderman* (Sam Raimi, 2002)

blocking: the placement of a character or an object partially behind another character or object. The camera shoots what is blocking in the foreground of the shot, and what is being blocked in the background of the shot.

■ Characters and objects are partially obscured in order to create meaning for the viewer.

■ *e.g.* An insecure or frightened character might be shot within a crowd, where only a fragment of the character can be seen. The character's anxious state of mind is relayed through the blocking.

blow-up: a process by which a still image or a frame from a film is enlarged, so that a particular detail is highlighted.

■ Blow-up shots are often used within the *marketing* of a film to create posters. A particular moment from a film can be blown up to be used on the film's poster and to create an expectation in the potential audience concerning the characters or action of the film.

blue screen/green screen: a type of special effect in which action is shot in front of a plain blue or green background. The plain background is then abstracted from the *footage*, allowing a different set of images to be inserted behind the original action.

■ *e.g.* Many of the scenes in which Kate Winslet and Leonardo DiCaprio appeared on the deck of the ship in *Titanic* (*James Cameron*, 1997) were shot in a studio, against a green screen, and were then digitally mapped onto the footage of the ship.

b

body double: an individual whose body is used instead of an actor's for a particular shot or scene.

■ For some shots, the director of a film may not consider the actor's body to be suitable for the effect desired. At this point a body double is used. Some actors have clauses built into their contracts which prohibit the director from asking them to appear naked in a scene. If this is the case, a body double is used.

body language: the movement of a character's face or body to suggest meaning.

■ The body language of a character can give the audience a lot of information, about the character's feelings, responses to other characters and position within the social structure of a film storyline.

Bollywood: the Indian film industry.

■ 'Bombay' and 'Hollywood' have been combined to produce the term 'Bollywood'. The film output of Bollywood is very high. Bollywood films use Indian actors, directors and crew.

boom: a long 'arm' on which a camera, microphone or light can be placed in order to position it effectively within a scene.

bootleg: an unofficial or pirate copy of a film, sold illegally.

■ Bootleg copies — usually of poor quality — often appear when a particular film has been banned or removed from distribution within a particular country.

box office: describes not only the place in a cinema where viewers buy tickets, but also the amount of money taken by an individual film.

■ The box-office success of a film is incredibly important to producers, but it is not the final step in making money from a film. Television distribution, video and DVD sales, as well as merchandise sales, also have a financial impact.

breakaway: a *prop* or a part of a *set* which has been especially designed to either break or come away from the set easily.

■ Breakaways are often used in action films, as they allow actors to perform fights or physical stunts without getting hurt.

bridging shot: a shot which shows a change in time or location and is used to connect one *scene* to another.

■ Bridging shots are often used to denote the passage of time. For example, a film might cut from a location at one time of year to the same location at another time of year in order to indicate that time has passed.

■ *e.g. Notting Hill* (Roger Michell, 1999) includes a sophisticated sequence of bridging shots in which the character played by Hugh Grant walks through the market in Notting Hill and as he does so the weather and people's clothing change in order to indicate the passing of a year.

British Academy of Film and Television Arts (BAFTA): the body which awards the British equivalent of the *Oscar*, known after the academy's acronym as the BAFTA.

British Board of Film Classification (BBFC): the organisation which allocates age-related *certificates* to films and videos in Britain.
- The BBFC is an independent, non-governmental body which not only allocates certificates but assesses films and videos before release and can cut material which it deems to be inappropriate. It has had responsibility for cinema regulation for more than 80 years and has overseen video certification since 1985.
- The British Board of Film Censors was established in 1912 to introduce some degree of uniformity into censorship. Prior to this, local authorities imposed their own, often wildly different, censorship standards. By the mid-1920s local authorities had accepted the need for a uniform code of censorship and it became general practice for them to accept the censorship decisions made by the board.
- The first appointed president of the BBFC was T. P. O'Connor, who drew up a list of 43 different criteria for the guidance of film examiners. This first list of BBFC criteria was very strict and included points concerning nudity, blasphemy, drunkenness, 'indecorous dancing', scenes suggestive of immorality and the exhibition of profuse bleeding. Today, the criteria which the BBFC uses in order to assess films for classification are different and concentrate more on images of extended/gratuitous violence, sexual violence and instructive practices (e.g. taking drugs and making bombs).

British New Wave: describes the films produced in Britain in the 1950s and 1960s by directors such as Lindsay Anderson and Tony Richardson.
- Called the British New Wave after the *French New Wave* films which were produced at the same time, the British New Wave shared its French counterpart's interest in experimental forms of camerawork and editing. It also used the same kind of amoral or problematic central character.
- *e.g.* *Look Back in Anger* (Tony Richardson, 1959), *A Taste of Honey* (Tony Richardson, 1961), *If...* (Lindsay Anderson, 1968)

buddy film: a type of film which centres on the friendship between two male characters.
- Buddy film was particularly in evidence in *Hollywood* cinema of the 1960s and 1970s, but has evolved to include relationships which are not always male or heterosexual e.g. *Thelma and Louise* (**Ridley Scott**, 1991), *The Adventures of Priscilla, Queen of the Desert* (Stephan Elliott, 1994).
- *e.g.* *Butch Cassidy and the Sundance Kid* (George Roy Hill, 1969)

b

Burton, Tim (1958–): film *director*.

■ Born in California, Burton worked for *Disney* before moving on to direct his own films. He is perhaps most famous for his dark, Gothic tales of the outsider figure who seems unable to find his place within society.

■ Filmography: *Vincent* (1982), *Pee-wee's Big Adventure* (1985), *Beetlejuice* (1988), *Batman* (1989), *Edward Scissorhands* (1990), *Batman Returns* (1992), *Ed Wood* (1994), *Mars Attacks!* (1996), *Sleepy Hollow* (1999), *Planet of the Apes* (2001)

Cahiers du Cinéma: a famous French film magazine, begun in 1951 by André Bazin.
■ The magazine included essays by *French New Wave* directors, such as Jean-Luc Godard and François Truffaut, about the changes which were occurring in French cinema and the direction in which French cinema should head.

call sheet: written information given to each cast and crew member at the end of a day's filming.
■ The call sheet includes the time each cast and crew member is needed on the next set, the scenes to be shot, the actors needed for each scene and the relevant locations.

cameo: a very short appearance in a film, often by a famous individual.
■ *e.g.* Alfred Hitchcock was famous for his brief cameos in his own films.

camera: the piece of equipment used to photograph images.
■ A camera consists of a *lens*, which projects the image onto the film stock; a shutter, which regulates the amount of light hitting the film; a viewfinder, which enables the camera operator to view the image during filming; a mechanism to propel the film through the camera during filming; a motor to power the camera; and a magazine, which holds the film before and after exposure.

camera angle: refers to the placement of the camera in relation to the main subject within the frame.
■ An eye-level shot is where the camera is positioned at chest or head height. This generates a sense of normality for the audience, who are used to viewing events from eye-level.
■ A *low-angle shot* positions the camera below eye level, looking up at a character, object or the action within a scene. This type of shot tends to make what is shot look powerful and even threatening.
■ A *high-angle shot* places the camera above eye level, looking down on the

characters or action. What the audience views therefore seems vulnerable or insignificant.

■ A *point-of-view shot* (POV) presents action as if from the viewpoint of a particular character. This can encourage the audience to identify with a character or empathise with his/her situation.

camera assistant: a member of the film crew who works with the director of photography and the camera operator.

■ The responsibilities of the camera assistant include maintaining and setting up the camera, changing lenses, loading film, measuring focus distances, focusing and zooming during the shot and keeping the camera reports.

camera car: a specially constructed vehicle containing a variety of mounts on which *cameras* can be placed.

■ Cameras can be mounted on the front, rear or side of the car. The vehicle being filmed is sometimes towed behind the camera car in order to make the scene appear more realistic and less jerky than if the camera car were driving in front of the car being filmed.

camera crew: the department on a film production which deals with all aspects of camera set-up, operation and organisation.

■ A camera crew consists of the director of photography, camera operators, a first *camera assistant* and a second camera assistant. The camera crew is responsible for the photography of the film and all aspects of camera equipment maintenance.

camera movement: the movement of the camera during filming. Either the camera is static and the 'head' of it moves or the whole camera moves. See also *dolly, panning, tilt* and *tracking shot*.

Cameron, James (1954–): film *director*.

■ Born in Ontario, Canada, Cameron spent his film apprenticeship with Roger Corman, as a set designer, miniature set builder and art director. He is perhaps most famous for the budgets of his films. *Titanic* was the first $200 million film. He is also closely associated with huge, epic tales of action, adventure and romance.

■ Filmography: *Piranha II* (1981), *The Terminator* (1984), *Aliens* (1986), *The Abyss* (1989), *Terminator 2: Judgement Day* (1991), *True Lies* (1994), *Titanic* (1997).

Campion, Jane (1954–): film *director*.

■ Born in Wellington, New Zealand, Campion trained at the Australian Film and Television School from 1981. The originality and stylistic artistry of her films have earned her a reputation as one of the best film directors of her generation. Originally only gaining small budgets, Campion can now command relatively

C

high budgets for films which still counter the formulaic products of Hollywood *mainstream cinema*.

■ Filmography: *Sweetie* (1989), *An Angel at My Table* (1990), *The Piano* (1993), *The Portrait of a Lady* (1997), *Holy Smoke* (1999)

Cannes Film Festival: French film festival, begun in 1946.

■ The Cannes festival shows new films and also gives awards to films and film-makers, such as the Palme D'Or for the best film.

canted framing: a camera angle which appears skewed or tilted to the viewer.

■ Canted angles are often used to create a disorientating effect for the audience of a film.

cartoons: short *animated* features.

■ Many cartoons were produced by the major *Hollywood* studios in the 1940s and 1950s.

■ *e.g.* The most famous of these include characters such as Bugs Bunny, Daffy Duck and Tom and Jerry.

cast: the group of people who play the characters in a film. Used as a verb, it means to select the performers for a film.

■ The *credits* at the beginning and end of a film will include cast details.

cause and effect: often used in the study of film to describe the movement of a story.

■ One event will occur within a film and provide the 'cause'. The 'effect' of the event is then seen either in the subsequent events or in the behaviour of a character.

■ *TIP* Most mainstream films work on a 'cause and effect' model. Stories move forwards via the presentation of events and their direct effects.

cel: a sheet of plastic on which individual images are drawn to create a piece of *animation*.

■ A single *cartoon* is made up of thousands of cells, each depicting a fractional change in the character or setting.

censorship: the process by which decisions are made as to whether a film, or scenes in it, are appropriate for the viewing public.

■ The *British Board of Film Classification* is the organisation that oversees film censorship in Britain.

■ *e.g.* Scenes depicting sexual and other violence were cut from *Oliver Stone*'s *Natural Born Killers* (1994) before it was given a certificate and a release in Britain.

■ *TIP* There have been occasions when a film has been censored by local councils or individuals rather than by the BBFC. Stanley Kubrick withdrew his film *A Clockwork Orange* from release in 1972 after a panic in the press. Even though it had been given a certificate by the BBFC, William Friedkin's *The Exorcist* was banned by numerous local councils in the early 1970s.

certificate: before a film can gain cinema or video release it must go through a process of certification by the *British Board of Film Classification*. This gives it a certificate indicating the age of the target viewer.

■ Film certificates have changed over the years. The 'X' certificate once used to denote films with adult content has now been replaced with the '18' rating. Certificates are issued on the basis of criteria regarding content, such as sex, violence, sexual violence, language and depictions of drug taking. For example, certain four-letter words can only appear once in a 12-certificate film. More than once and the film will be given a 15 certificate.

César: the French equivalent to the *Oscar*.

CGI: see *computer-generated imagery*.

character: a person or animal (animated or otherwise) who exists within the story of a film.
■ Films can be described as 'character driven', which means that the storyline revolves around the experiences of the main characters.

character actor: an actor who is often seen playing minor roles. The same type of role is repeated across a number of different films.
■ Often the characters played by this type of actor are unusual, quirky or unattractive.

character theme: the part of a *sound track* which is associated with a particular character.
■ *TIP* Character themes might be used to introduce characters into a scene or to indicate their status within a scene. If the character theme of one character is evident, but he or she is no longer in the scene, it can also be used to suggest the presence of the character in the mind of another character.
■ *e.g.* John Williams's famous music for *Jaws* (*Steven Spielberg*, 1975) became the character theme for the shark in the film. It is played to signify the presence of the shark, even when this 'character' is not on the screen.

chiaroscuro lighting: describes highly contrasting lighting, which gives deep shadows and bright highlights.
■ Chiaroscuro lighting is often used to generate atmosphere and tone within a scene. It can arouse a sense of suspicion, fear or concern in the viewer.

chick flick: describes films which are aimed at a female audience.
■ The term does not indicate a feminist film, but one which has some level of

C

discussion concerning female experience and is targeted at a wide, mainstream female audience.

■ *e.g.* *Bridget Jones's Diary* (Sharon Maguire, 2000)

choreography: the composition of dance steps or action sequences within films.

■ *e.g.* The director *John Woo* is renowned for his highly choreographed action sequences in films such as *Face/Off* (1997).

Cinematograph Act 1909: government legislation, specifically relating to film, passed in 1909.

■ The Cinematograph Act was the first piece of film-related legislation to be passed. It introduced the licensing of cinemas and was originally conceived to enforce fire regulations. Under the Cinematograph Act, statutory control lay with local authorities. The 'birth' of the *British Board of Film Classification* (under a slightly different name) in 1912, standardised decisions made by the local councils.

Cinematograph Act 1952: government legislation, specifically relating to film, passed in order to update the *Cinematograph Act 1909*.

■ This act prohibited children from watching 'unsuitable films', advised local authorities to instruct cinemas in their areas not to show films unless they had a certificate, and stipulated that advertising for specific films must indicate age restrictions.

cinematographer: the person responsible for camerawork and lighting on a film.

■ The cinematographer is sometimes referred to as the director of photography.

■ *e.g.* Conrad Hall was a famous cinematographer. His films included *American Beauty* (1999) and *Road to Perdition* (2002).

cinematography: the work on a film done by a *cinematographer*, such as deciding on camera angles, lens types and colour balances.

clapper board: a hinged slate which displays the name of a film, its director, the date and the scene number.

■ The two hinged parts of the clapper board are 'clapped' together at the beginning of a scene. This is done to synchronise the commencement of lighting, sound and camera needed for a scene.

cliffhanger: a scene or film ending which does not resolve events but leaves questions in the viewer's mind.

■ Cliffhangers are often used to generate tension and suspense.

clip: a short section of a film shown on its own.

C

closed set: a film set or location which is closed to everyone but key personnel.
■ A set might be closed when a delicate or explicit scene is being shot, either to give the actors some privacy or in order to generate speculation (e.g. among the press) about what is being shot.

close-up: a camera shot of a person or object taken at close range.
■ A close-up of a character is often of his/her face in order to relay information about the character's emotions to the viewer.

closure: relates to storytelling, which describes the bringing together of all the questions and loose ends within a film to provide final answers.
■ Closure allows viewers to feel satisfied that they have been given a conclusion to their viewing experience.

Coen Brothers: directing and producing team of two brothers.
■ Joel Coen was born in 1954 and Ethan Coen in 1957, both in Minnesota, USA. They have become best known for independent, quirky and original films which often avoid straight *genre* definition. They write, direct and produce many of their films, and have won critical acclaim, including two *Oscars* for *Fargo* (1996).
■ Filmography: *Blood Simple* (1985), *Raising Arizona* (1987), *Miller's Crossing* (1990), *Barton Fink* (1991), *The Hudsucker Proxy* (1994), *Fargo* (1996), *The Big Lebowski* (1998), *Oh Brother, Where Art Thou?* (2000), *The Man Who Wasn't There* (2001).

Colorisation: a computer-aided process in which colour is added to black and white film.
■ Colorisation has been widely criticised for making assumptions about the colours which would have been used if colour technology had been available at the time of filming. It is also charged with losing the tones, which may have been of great significance, in the original black and white film.

colour: an important element in the generation of tone, atmosphere and meaning.
■ Colours which appear dominant in scenes or those attached to people and objects can be used to great effect within films.
■ *e.g.* Consider the startling colour change when Dorothy enters the land of Oz in *The Wizard of Oz* (1939). Her 'real' life is depicted in black and white, but her fantasy world is in *Technicolor*, bringing out the escapism and dream quality of Oz. The colour red becomes significant in Steven Spielberg's *Schindler's List* (1993), as the red of a young girl's coat is highlighted against the black and white of the rest of the scene. When viewers see a flash of red within a mound of bodies, the plight of the girl under the Nazi regime is horribly evoked.

C

comedy film: a film which treats its subject matter in a humorous way.
- There are many different types of comedy film, including black, *romantic*, *screwball* and *slapstick*.

commentary: a voice that can be heard by the viewer and not by those in the film, which offers some explanation of events being presented.
- The word 'commentary' is mostly used to describe the voice heard in a documentary film. For commentaries in fictional films, see *voice-over*.

compositing: the *special effects* process of combining two images that could not ordinarily be combined.
- The process of compositing can now be performed using digital technology. Backgrounds can be filmed and then combined with action shots to form a single image.

composition: the arrangement of a *scene* during the filming process.
- The composition of a particular scene is decided by the director, who makes decisions concerning camera angles, camera movement and the movement of characters.

computer-generated imagery (CGI): images which have been created on a computer and then added to a film.
- CGI has been used to create entire films or parts of films. Some films use CGI to recreate elements (such as unreal or fantasy aspects) which would otherwise be too expensive to produce. Other films might be remastered by adding CGI elements.
- The process of generating a computer image often begins with the skeleton of the shape to be animated. In *Jurassic Park* (Steven Spielberg, 1993) the Industrial Light and Magic (ILM) animators began by building dinosaur skeletons in their computers. They found pictures of bones and scanned them to achieve a realistic dinosaur shape. Anatomically accurate models were also built and then scanned using a Cyberware scanner, which focuses a revolving laser beam on its subject, so obtaining information from all angles and all depths. The next stage was to 'fit' the information from the scanner over the skeleton already created in the computer. The T-Rex dinosaur was produced in this way. Once its movements had been created in the computer, using knowledge of its shape and size plus the information gained through moving the models to predict how it would move, the dinosaur came to life on the screen.
- *e.g.* CGI was used to create the cityscapes of Rome in *Gladiator* (*Ridley Scott*, 2000) and to create many shots of the ship and its passengers in *Titanic* (*James Cameron*, 1997). Jabba the Hut, the character from the original *Star Wars* trilogy, was created in CGI for the re-release of the films and this creation was then added to the original footage. The dinosaurs of *Jurassic Park* and the

C

character of Gollum from *The Lord of the Rings: The Two Towers* (Peter Jackson, 2002) are CGI creations. *Shrek* (Andrew Adamson, 2001), *Toy Story* (John Lasseter, 1995) and *Monsters Inc.* (Peter Doctor, 2001) are notable examples of films created purely with CGI.

connotation: describes the meanings that words, images and sounds generate which are beyond their literal meanings.
■ The meanings viewers read into a film can be affected by their age, gender and cultural background. The connotations of a particular image, object, setting or gesture may therefore be different for different viewers.
■ *e.g.* For some viewers a red rose is a symbol of love or romance. For someone interested in politics it might be read as a symbol of the Labour party. For a viewer who has sporting interests, the rose might imply rugby.

contextualisation: the process of placing a film within a historical era or in relation to other films.
■ Studies are sometimes made of the historical context of a film and of how the attitudes which existed at that time affect the film's story and characters. Alternatively, a film by a particular director may be studied in the context of other films by that director, with attention to similarities or differences. It is also possible to study films made by a particular studio or production company and comment on how these other films relate to the one in focus.

continuity editing: editing which aims to create a sense of realism. The film text is organised so that the *narrative* moves in a linear and chronological manner.
■ Continuity editing is most closely associated with *mainstream cinema*, which aims to create narratives that approximate the movement of real time. Events are organised so as not to disorientate the viewer.
■ *e.g. Ridley Scott*'s *Gladiator* (2000) follows the story of the central protagonist from his initial glory, through personal tragedy and hardship, to his eventual revenge and death.
■ *TIP* Continuity edited films may include *flashback* and *flash forward* narrative devices, but these do not interrupt the forward momentum of the chronology.

continuity sheet: information concerning the number of takes, shots, camera positions, angles, lenses, settings, lighting set-ups, costume changes and actors needed for each day's shooting.
■ The continuity sheet is essential for the cast and crew of a film, as it enables them to prepare everything which is needed for a particular shot.

contrapuntal sound: refers to sound which does not seem to 'fit' with the scene or images you are watching.
■ *e.g.* The song 'Over the Rainbow' is used in *John Woo*'s film *Face/Off* (1997) in a shoot-out scene. It seems contradictory to the violence of the scene, but

is actually being used to calm a frightened boy. The song begins as *diegetic sound* in the child's headphones, but spills out onto the *non-diegetic* sound track as if to highlight the innocence and vulnerability of the boy in such an environment. The scene of Renton in his squalid room, attempting to give up 'junk' in Danny Boyle's *Trainspotting* (1995), is accompanied by a sound track of classical music. This seeming contradiction of tone allows for an even greater degree of comparison between the affluent world often associated with classical music and the drug-addicted deprivation of Renton's life.

convention: a frequently used element which becomes standard in a group of films.

■ Categories or *genres* of films share a group of conventions which they all use.

■ *e.g. Horror films* invariably use conventions of the frightening place, the 'monster' and the final girl (left to confront and overcome the killer after all her friends have been killed).

■ *TIP* Although films within a certain category will all use some of the conventions available to them, they will not always use the same convention in the same way. The 'monster' in horror films might be supernatural, a creature or a psychotic human being.

Coppola, Francis Ford (1939–): film *director*.

■ Born in Detroit, USA, Coppola studied film at UCLA and has had a career so far spanning 40 years. He has either directed or been associated with some of the most famous examples of films in contemporary cinema. He is a huge figure in *Hollywood* and is accorded more freedom by studios than many of his fellow directors.

■ Filmography: *The Playgirls and the Bellboy* (1962), *Dementia 13* (1963), *You're a Big Boy Now* (1966), *Finian's Rainbow* (1968), *The Rain People* (1969), *The Godfather* (1972), *The Godfather Part II* (1974), *Apocalypse Now* (1979), *One from the Heart* (1982), *The Outsiders* (1983), *Rumble Fish* (1983), *The Cotton Club* (1984), *Peggy Sue Got Married* (1986), *Gardens of Stone* (1987), *Tucker: The Man and His Dream* (1988), *The Godfather Part III* (1990), *Bram Stoker's Dracula* (1992), *Jack* (1996), *The Rainmaker* (1997), *Apocalypse Now Redux* (2001), *Megalopolis* (2003)

co-production: a film produced with the backing of more than one production company.

■ Many films are co-productions because they cannot gain the funding they require from one source only.

costume: the clothes which the actors wear in a film.

■ The costumes used in a film are important in the creation of historical time, the evocation of characters' states of mind and status, and the generation of place.

C

■ *e.g.* The differing clothes worn in each of the three time periods in Stephen Daldry's *The Hours* (2002), clearly define the 1920s, the 1940s and the 1990s. Changes in costume for a particular character during a film can indicate anything from a change in fortune to a shift in political affiliation. Julia Roberts's costume shift in *Pretty Woman* (1990) carries particular meaning and signals the movement of her character from street hustling prostitute to girlfriend of a tycoon. Within this kind of Cinderella story the shedding of one set of clothes and the adoption of another signals a change in social status.

costume drama: a film set in a particular period of history, using the costume of that period.

■ These films are often based on a work of literature or the life of a famous historical figure.

■ *e.g.* Sense and Sensibility (*Ang Lee*, 1995)

cover shot: extra *footage* which is taken during the filming process and covers all the scenes which are shot.

■ Cover shots are especially important at the *editing* stage of a film, when the director might realise that an image essential to the film has not been filmed with the other main footage. In this situation, a cover shot can be used to fill in the gap.

crab dolly: a four-wheeled device on which a camera can be mounted, allowing the filming of complicated moving shots. Crab dollies cannot be used for *tracking shots*.

crab shot: a camera shot which places the camera in a limited or enclosed space.
■ If a director wishes to shoot under a bed or within a cupboard, for example, a crab shot might be used.

crane shot: a type of shot filmed from a crane, which creates a *high angle*.
■ The crane is a piece of equipment which places the camera on an arm and allows it to be lifted into the air.

credits: the information at the beginning and the end of a film which gives details of *cast*, *crew*, *distribution* and *producers*.

■ The credits at the beginning of a film are usually placed over the images of the film's opening sequence. Credits at the end are much longer and are often placed over a dark screen.

crew: the individuals who take part in the technical side of the film-making process.

■ The crew for a film includes the director, cinematographer, editor, runner and anybody else who has helped make the film. The actors in a film are called the *cast*.

critic: an individual who writes about a film, shortly after release, and reviews the content, character and other details.

■ Film critics review the acting within a film as well as its directorial style and potential audience impact. They can have a significant effect on a film's eventual success or failure at the *box office*.

■ *e.g.* There are many film critics writing today for newspapers as well as film magazines such as *Sight and Sound, Empire, Total Film* and *Premiere.* Derek Malcolm's column for the *Observer* is particularly well regarded.

Cronenberg, David (1943–): film *director*.

■ Born in Toronto, Canada, Cronenberg was educated at the University of Toronto. He is most famous for his 'body horror' films in which the human body is invaded by another entity or organism and taken over. He is fascinated with the power of germs and viruses to use the human body as a host in which they can thrive. His films are as much *science fiction* as *horror*, and often contain characters whose motivations and actions are strange, perverse or anti-social. Cronenberg's cinematic vision is very much his own and is translated into his films with little influence from producers or studios.

■ Filmography: *Stereo* (1969), *Crimes of the Future* (1970), *Shivers* (1975), *Rabid* (1976), *Fast Company* (1979), *The Brood* (1979), *Scanners* (1980), *Videodrome* (1982), *The Dead Zone* (1983), *The Fly* (1986), *Dead Ringers* (1988), *Naked Lunch* (1991), *M. Butterfly* (1993), *Crash* (1996), *eXistenZ* (1999), *Spider* (2002)

cropping: the process by which the outer sections of an image are cut away.

■ Cropping might be used to get rid of unwanted images which were part of a shot and are unnecessary to the film.

cross-cut: the process of *editing* from one *scene* to another and then usually back to the original scene.

■ A film might cross-cut to many scenes in order to give information to the viewer concerning the relationship of one scene to another or of characters to one another. Cross-cutting is used to show events happening at the same time in different locations.

crowd scene: a scene which involves many individuals.

■ Crowd scenes can be used for a number of different purposes, e.g. to indicate the response of a large group of people to an event or development involving a main character. *Extras* are regularly engaged to participate in crowd scenes.

■ *e.g.* The crowd scenes in *Ridley Scott's Gladiator* (2000) were used to indicate the scale of Rome and the response of the Colosseum crowd to the central character.

cult film: a film which does not have a wide audience or even wide release, but which does have a select group of avid followers.

C

■ *e.g. The Rocky Horror Picture Show* (Jim Sharman, 1975) still has a cult following of fans who dress as the characters at screenings and re-enact the dance routines from the film in the aisles.

cut: the most common way of connecting images within a film. One image changes directly into another.

■ Cuts are a form of invisible *editing,* in that the viewer does not consciously notice the shift from one image to another. In this way, a sense of realism can be retained by the film. Cuts are the most common form of edit within *continuity editing.*

cutaway: a brief shot of something which is outside the main *scene.*

■ Cutaways might be to a different location, or to a character or object not in the main scene. They are often used in order to relay information concerning a character's thoughts or state of mind.

cut back: a term used in *editing* to describe the movement back to the main action from a different viewpoint or image.

cut-in shot: a shot which cuts into a small part of the main scene.

■ The cut-in shot might be to a significant detail in the scene, such as a clue or a weapon. This type of shot allows the film-maker to highlight significant details within a scene for the viewer.

dailies: the outcome of each day's shooting, used by the *director* and *cinematographer* to check camera set-ups and lighting.

decor: refers to the colours, furniture and overall look of rooms in a film.
- The rooms in which the action of a scene occurs can add meaning to the event shown. The decor of a room can also mirror a character's psychological state.
- *e.g.* Norman Bates's study in Hitchcock's *Psycho* (1960) is full of old furniture and stuffed birds — the decor has no vitality; it is devoid of life, almost mummified. The rooms on different decks in *James Cameron*'s *Titanic* (1997) present the class differences between the passengers. The upper decks are opulent and expensively furnished. The rooms for lower-class passengers are simple and functional.

deep focus: a type of camerawork which allows action taking place near and far away from the camera to be equally clear.
- Deep focus allows the viewer to see each part of a shot clearly and can therefore be useful in enabling the director to make everything within a particular shot potentially significant.
- *e.g.* Orson Welles's 1941 classic *Citizen Kane* used deep focus photography to comment on the relationships between all the characters and objects which were on the screen.

denotation: describes the literal meaning of what can be seen or heard.
- If the numbers 1999 appeared on the screen, a date would instantly be denoted to the viewer. The associations which the viewer might have with that particular date would be among its *connotations*.

denouement: the moment in a film when all the mysteries are solved and all the questions are answered for the audience.
- The tension or complexities of a film might be resolved in a denouement scene, in which a character explains a mystery or an event happens which makes sense of previous uncertainties. Such scenes contribute to a film's *closure*.

■ *e.g.* In a thriller, the identity of the criminal or killer is often revealed during a denouement scene.

depth of field: the area either behind or in front of the main subject of a shot, which is still in clear *focus* for the audience.

■ The director of photography and the director make decisions concerning the depth of field required within a shot. They may decide that the focus should rest purely on the subject of the shot and then make camera decisions accordingly. Alternatively, they may decide that all parts of the shot hold important information for the viewer, in which case the field may be very deep and may include all parts of the shot.

detective film: a type of film in which a detective (either a member of the police force or an independent investigator) works towards solving a crime by a process of detailed investigation.

■ The detective frequently has a 'sidekick' who helps solve the crimes but has far fewer skills of detection. Detective films often draw directly on novels which have a detection narrative.

■ *e.g.* Sir Arthur Conan Doyle's stories about the detective Sherlock Holmes have provided the basis for many detective films, notably *The Hound of the Baskervilles* (Sidney Lanfield, 1939).

diachronic narrative: a term used in semiotics and critical theory to describe a forward movement of time.

■ In film studies, a diachronic narrative is one in which events progress chronologically and there is no fragmentation of time. Most *mainstream* films follow a diachronic narrative pattern in order not to break the audience's attention.

diagonal action: action which takes place across the screen, seemingly from one corner to another.

■ Diagonal action is traditionally used to create a sense of dynamic action.

diegesis: literally, 'story'.

■ In a film the diegesis is the fictional world in which the events occur. The characters, music, props, locations and objects of this world are all part of the film's diegesis.

diegetic sound: sound which the characters within a film can hear.

■ Diegetic sound can include everything from traffic, industrial machinery, telephones, doors slamming and music to animal noises and dialogue. These sounds may be used to generate a reality effect for the audience (see *realism*), but can also take on symbolic meaning.

■ *e.g.* The perpetual rain of the metropolis in *David Fincher*'s film *Se7en* (1995) creates a constant backdrop to the action of the film as well as coming to represent the inhospitable nature of the city. Diegetic sounds can also become synonymous with particular characters and act to signal their presence in a film. In *Scream* (Wes Craven, 1996) the killer(s) harass their victims via the telephone. The opening image of the film is of a phone ringing and the character who answers it becomes the first victim. From then on the sound of a phone ringing becomes associated with the disjointed voice of the killer(s) contacting their next victim. This everyday and banal sound thus becomes threatening and creates tension for the audience.

■ *TIP* Be aware that directors can also put sounds you would expect to hear in the story world on the *sound track*. They may do this in order to heighten the tension in a particular scene or suggest a connection between one scene and another.

digital camera: a type of camera which records images digitally so that they can be downloaded onto a computer.

■ Digital cameras are increasingly superseding *analogue* equipment in the film-making process. They are often smaller, lighter and more easy to manipulate than standard 35 mm cameras.

■ *e.g.* The latest *Star Wars* instalment, *Attack of the Clones* (George Lucas, 2002), was shot using digital cameras.

diorama: see *big-screen cinema*.

director: the member of the crew who has ultimate control over the entire shooting of a film.

■ The director will work closely with the *cinematographer*, *editor* and *producer* in order to oversee the look of the final film product.

director's viewfinder: a device which allows the director to see the shot he/she wants to shoot, without having to use a camera.

■ A standard viewfinder helps the director to decide which camera and which lens is needed for a shot.

disaster film: a film in which the story revolves around a central disastrous event.

■ Disaster films have been popular at the *box office* for a number of years. They are often big budget, rely heavily on *special effects* technologies and are sold on dramatic events as much as on cast.

■ *e.g.* *The Towering Inferno* (John Guillermin, 1974), *Titanic* (*James Cameron*, 1997), *Dante's Peak* (Roger Donaldson, 1997), *Armageddon* (Michael Bay, 1998), *Deep Impact* (Mimi Leder, 1998)

discourse: a set of statements connected with a particular experience or field; a discussion taking place within a set structure.

d

■ Film theory includes a number of different discourses which share a set of critical ideas and statements. *Feminist film* theory is an example of a discourse which has its own language and critical framework.

disequilibrium: the period of instability within a film's story.

■ In many types of film, the stable or safe situation presented at the beginning of the story (see *equilibrium*) is disrupted by forces which bring about a state of disequilibrium. The destabilising forces can come in the form of characters or events. Periods of disequilibrium are necessary for a film because they generate tension for the viewer, who then wants to see how the now complicated events are resolved in the *denouement*.

■ *e.g.* At the beginning of *Ridley Scott*'s *Alien* (1979) the crew of the *Nostromo* are bored but safe; with the arrival of the alien there is excitement but mortal danger. It is left to Sigourney Weaver's Ripley character to reinstate safety and end the period of disequilibrium by killing the alien.

Disney: the studio famous for animated productions, named after its founder Walt Disney.

■ Disney has become a brand name and is associated with theme parks and merchandise, as well as films. Recent Disney productions have employed *computer-generated imagery* rather than traditional *animation*.

■ *e.g.* *Snow White and the Seven Dwarfs* (1937), *Bambi* (1942) and *Cinderella* (1950) are all examples of early Disney films which helped to create the studio's reputation, while recent films using CGI include *Beauty and the Beast* (Gary Trousdale, 1991) and *The Haunted Mansion* (Rob Minkhoff, 2003).

dissolve: a type of *editing* where one image gradually *fades* and the next appears. For a brief time, the two images can be seen simultaneously.

■ Dissolves are often used to indicate a relationship or a connection between the two scenes or images which are seen dissolving into each other.

distribution: the process by which a finished film is sent out to cinemas to be screened.

■ It is the job of the distributor to make sure that a film gains maximum exposure by being shown in as many contexts (initially cinema, and later video and DVD) as possible.

docudrama: a film that dramatises real-life events.

■ As in a *biopic*, the events shown in a docudrama may be treated with some cinematic licence and be made more dramatic and crowd-pleasing than they originally were, but the main events in the film will actually have occurred.

■ *e.g.* *In the Name of the Father* (Jim Sheridan, 1993), a film about the life of Gerry Conlon, which dramatises his wrongful arrest for IRA terrorist activities and *Dance with a Stranger* (Mike Newell, 1985), a film about the events leading up to the hanging of Ruth Ellis

documentary: a film which presents the actual events which happen in a real-life context.

■ *e.g.* The documentary director John Grierson is often cited as the 'father' of British documentary with his work in the 1930s.

dolly: a platform on wheels, on which a camera can be placed in order to allow more freedom of movement during filming. Dollies can be used for *tracking shots*.

double bill: two, often related, films shown during one cinema 'sitting'.

■ It is rare today to see cinemas advertising double bills. During the earlier days of cinema, double bills provided a popular evening's entertainment, often consisting of a *B-movie* followed by the main feature.

dubbing: the process by which *sound* is added to a film, usually in the form of a different language dubbed over the original language.

■ Dubbing is not only used for translation. Occasionally (especially for singing) an actor's voice is dubbed with that of another in the same language.

■ *e.g.* Andy McDowell's voice was dubbed with that of Glenn Close in the film *Greystoke: The Legend of Tarzan, Lord of the Apes* (Hugh Hudson, 1984).

Dutch angle: a type of *camera angle* which does not use regular vertical or horizontal lines.

■ The camera might be tipped to one side in a Dutch angle shot or be positioned so as to generate the effect of looking at something from a very odd angle. Dutch angles are often used to generate a disconcerting effect and make the audience uneasy.

DVD (digital versatile disc): a form of film-viewing technology which is rapidly replacing VHS video.

■ DVDs have seven times the capacity of a standard compact disc and are therefore able to hold far more than just a film text. They often include scene analyses, *storyboards, behind-the-scenes footage*, plus cast interviews and directors' commentaries providing insights into different 'readings' of the film. They offer the viewer a more varied package and a different viewing experience. When films were first available on DVD, the quality of the images and sound was often poor, but today's DVDs achieve standards which exceed those of VHS. For the industry, DVDs have now become a lucrative format, supplementing the revenue from VHS. Consumers who originally purchased films on VHS may buy the same films on DVD (just as some music-lovers own the same albums on vinyl and compact disc).

dystopia: describes a future or alternative world which is dysfunctional and problematic.

■ Dystopias are usually seen within the *science fiction* genre and serve as a warning to the audience of what the future might hold. Dystopic worlds are often those where technology has taken over or where man's obsession with progress has caused an apocalyptic event, such as a nuclear war.

■ *e.g. James Cameron*'s science fiction/*action film Terminator 2* (1991) includes images of a future world where technology has advanced beyond man and the machines have taken over.

■ *TIP* Note that dystopian futures are much more common than *utopian* ones in science fiction. If the future world is inhumane or ruled by technology, the challenge to the protagonist is much more dramatic.

Ealing Studios: a British film studio which produced films between 1931 and 1955.

■ It takes its name from the area of West London in which it was located.

■ *e.g.* Ealing Studios was perhaps most renowned for producing the 'Ealing Comedies'. Films such as *The Lavender Hill Mob* (Charles Crichton, 1951) were among the most popular and acclaimed of these.

editing: the process of gathering all the material completed during a film shot and placing it in an order which produces meaning most effectively for the viewer. See also *continuity editing* and *montage editing*.

editor: the member of a film-making team who organises the filmed *footage* into the correct order.

■ The editor often works closely with the *director* during the editing process.

18: a level of film classification which indicates that no one under the age of 18 should either see or rent a particular film. The *British Board of Film Classification* states that it rarely intervenes in the content of 18 films because it respects the right of adults to 'choose their own entertainment'.

■ The criteria which the British Board of Film Classification uses in order to assess films for an 18 certificate are:
  • Violent or dangerous acts are not shown in such a way as to promote such acts or give instructions on illegal activities.
  • Extremely explicit images of sexual activity are only allowed if fully justified by the context.

ellipsis: a section of time within a film which the viewer does not see but knows has passed.

■ An ellipsis is often used to 'squash' time, so that in the 2 or so hours of a film, only the most relevant visual information is offered to the viewer.

■ *e.g.* The words 'ten years later' provide an indication to the audience that an ellipsis has taken place.

e

enigma: a question, puzzle or mystery posed within a film's *narrative*.

■ The enigma of a film might come in the form of a hidden identity or motive. *Thrillers* and *horror films* often have an enigma at the heart of their narratives, which has to be clarified by the hero or heroine.

■ *e.g.* Norman Bates is only revealed as the killer in Hitchcock's *Psycho* (1960) at the end of the narrative. The audience is made to wait for the enigma to be cleared up, and this generates tension and *suspense*.

epic: a film which often has a huge *cast*, is set over a number of years and deals with grand themes, such as love and death.

■ Epics can be from any *genre*, but are distinguishable from other examples of that genre by scale. They are often based upon dramatised historical or biblical events.

■ *e.g.* *The Ten Commandments* (Cecil B. DeMille, 1956), *Gladiator* (*Ridley Scott*, 2000)

equilibrium: the secure, calm and balanced state which often exists at the beginning of a film's narrative.

■ The equilibrium of a film is often disrupted by negative forces or characters (see *disequilibrium*) and the remainder of the film is a journey for the characters and the viewer towards a renewed state of equilibrium and *closure*.

■ *e.g.* The peaceful (if somewhat dull) equilibrium which exists at the beginning of the *Coen Brothers'* film *Fargo* (1996) is disrupted by the presence of the two kidnappers. It is left to Francis McDormand's character, Police Chief Margie Gunderson, to resolve the chaos caused by the kidnappers and restore equilibrium.

Equity: an actors' union which exists in the United States and in Britain. Actors can only participate in professional acting (in the UK and in the US) if in possession of an Equity card.

establishing shot: this is usually a *long shot* or *extreme long shot* which introduces the viewer to a place within a film.

■ The establishing shot is so called because it establishes the place and time of the film's narrative, as well as the tone of the film. It rarely involves the central characters, but introduces viewers to the environment in which the majority of the action will take place.

■ *e.g.* The establishing shot in Anthony Minghella's *The English Patient* (1996) is an *aerial shot* of a plane flying over the desert. The desert environment is thus introduced as significant within the plot — and, indeed, it later provides the place where the lovers meet.

exhibition: the screening of a film in a cinema.

■ Appropriate and adequate exhibition is crucial to a film's success. The *multiplex* cinemas which have become a common context for film exhibition tend to show more *mainstream* (often *Hollywood*) films. For a lower-budget film production which does not have the advertising budget of a *blockbuster*, multiplex exhibition might be more difficult. Chain cinemas are profit-orientated businesses and show films which they can rely on for *box office* success. A lower-budget film may receive art-house exhibition, but this is not guaranteed.

expectations: the set of ideas which members of an audience have about a film before they go to view it.

■ Audience expectations can be satisfied if a film includes predictable elements, follows *conventions* for the *genre* or meets the same standards as its director's previous productions. If a film exceeds expectations or challenges them in an interesting way, this will add to the pleasure of the viewing experience.

exploitation film: a film which uses a current issue or subject and sensation-alises it for cinematic effect.

■ Exploitation films do not add useful debate to a contemporary issue, but merely use the issue to produce a sensational effect. Deciding whether a film is exploitative or not is affected by the date of release of the film and the attitudes of the viewer. *B-movies* which 'copy' the content and format of mainstream hits are often described as exploitation films.

■ *e.g.* Examples of films widely agreed to fall into the 'exploitation' category include the B-movie *I Walked with a Zombie* (RKO, 1943) and *Halloween: The Curse of Michael Myers* (Joe Chappelle, 1995).

expressionism: a style of cinema in which *lighting*, *colour* and *camera angles* are used to reflect the mood or thoughts of a character.

■ Expressionist films do not aim for *realism*, but rather seek to evoke mood, emotion and state of mind.

■ *e.g.* The German expressionist classic directed by Robert Wiene, *The Cabinet of Dr Caligari* (1919), uses different strengths and tones of light to create a *horror* mood and to reflect the fear of the characters.

extra: a person who is not a professional actor, but is hired to be part of a crowd scene.

extreme close-up: a camera shot which focuses on close detail.

■ Extreme close-ups (ECUs) are often used to present small but significant details to the viewer.

■ *e.g. David Lynch's* film *Blue Velvet* (1986) opens with a *tracking shot* of a suburban community, which then moves to an extreme close-up of a severed ear. The idea of the potential violence which exists below the white picket fence surface of suburban America is thus clearly indicated to the viewer.

extreme long shot: a type of camera shot which shows extreme distances, often featuring tiny human figures.

■ This type of shot, sometimes employed as an *establishing shot*, is generally used to indicate the vulnerability of characters within an overwhelming environment. See also *long shot*.

eye-level shot: where the camera is positioned at chest or head height. This generates a sense of normality for viewers, who are used to viewing events from eye level.

eyeline match: a type of edit which cuts from a character to what that character is looking at.

■ The level of the character's eyeline is maintained in the next shot by the positioning of another character or an object at the same level on the screen.

fade: an edit type in which an image gradually fades out to white or black.
■ A fade is often used to signal the end of a scene or film.

fantasy film: a film which includes a storyline and images which could not exist in the real world.
■ Fantasy films feature elements which could never be real, not even in the future.
■ *e.g.* Many of the films created with the animated models of Ray Harryhausen, such as *Jason and the Argonauts* (Don Chaffey, 1963), are examples of fantasy films. The storylines feature characters and locations drawn from Greek mythology.

feature film: any full-length film shown at the cinema.
■ The term used to be applied to the main film within a *double bill* and indicated its longer length and greater status.

feminist criticism: the body of critical study which examines the position of female characters within film, the representations of the female gender which are offered to the viewer and the position of women within the film industry.
■ Many approaches come under the main heading of feminist criticism, including criticism from a psychoanalytical and a racial perspective.
■ *e.g.* The writings of critics such as Laura Mulvey and Claire Johnston in the 1970s are often cited as the starting point for the type of feminist criticism which we see today. Mulvey's 1975 essay, 'Visual pleasure and narrative cinema', employed psychoanalytical ideas in order to analyse the way women were represented in film. The principal argument of her essay was that *mainstream cinema* was organised around a series of gazes constructed for male pleasure: camerawork, storylines and characterisation positioned the female characters as the object of the gaze.

feminist film: a film which specifically sets out to discuss women's experiences and issues connected with the female gender.

■ Feminist films differ from those which merely feature women in central roles as they overtly discuss issues of gender. Compare to *chick flick*.

■ *e.g.* the works of film directors such as Maya Deren and Chantal Akerman

femme fatale: a female character who uses her sexual power to trap male characters.

■ The *femme fatale* is a standard character within many types of film, including film noir. She draws the male character into the intrigues in the plot and controls his actions. The male characters who are manipulated by the *femme fatale* often come to a very sticky end.

■ *e.g.* The *femmes fatales* played by Barbara Stanwick in *Double Indemnity* (Billy Wilder, 1944) and Kathleen Turner in *Body Heat* (Lawrence Kasdan, 1981) draw the male characters into the crimes they want committed. John Dahl's 1990s *film noir, The Last Seduction,* brings the *femme fatale* into absolutely central focus, showing Bridget (Linda Fiorentino) as having absolute power over the man she chooses to manipulate.

15: a level of film classification which stipulates that no one younger than 15 years old should see a particular film at the cinema or rent the video.

■ The criteria which the *British Board of Film Classification* uses in order to assess films for a 15 certificate are:
  • All themes can be tackled, as long as the treatment of the theme is appropriate to 15-year-olds.
  • There may be frequent use of strong language, although prolonged, aggressive use of strong language is not acceptable.
  • There are no constraints on nudity, if in a non-sexual context.
  • Sexual activity can be represented, but without explicit detail.
  • Violence can be strong, but must not focus on the infliction of pain.
  • Dangerous fighting/combat techniques are not allowed; neither are scenes which emphasise the use of accessible lethal weapons such as knives.
  • Most horror techniques are allowed, but the sustained infliction of pain or injury is not.
  • Drug taking may be shown, but details of how to take drugs are not permitted.

fill light: a type of light which helps to soften harsh shadows which might be thrown by other lights used.

■ The fill (or filler) light is an important tool on a film set, because it helps to provide naturalistic lighting for a scene.

film festival: an event designed to show and promote films. It often includes elements of competition between films.

■ *e.g.* the *Cannes Film Festival,* the Venice Film Festival and the *Sundance Film Festival* (USA)

film form: describes the shape or structure of a film.

■ The analysis of film form includes all features of structure and shape which are used to create meaning within a film text.

■ The structure and shape of a film include the type of *narrative* and the micro elements (mise-en-scène, *editing*, *sound* and *cinematography*) which are used to create different meanings for the viewer. The type (or *genre*) of a film is also important within the analysis of film form, because the *conventions* used within a particular genre inform what the film looks like on the screen.

■ *e.g.* The 'false ending', where the killer is thought to be dead but comes back for one last attempted attack, a convention of the horror film, is an aspect of film form.

film noir: a French term, literally meaning 'black film', used to describe a style of film in which the events are dark and corrupt and the lighting casts atmospheric shadows.

■ The style of a *film noir* is distinctive, because lighting, props and settings are all used to evoke a menacing atmosphere. The story within a *film noir* usually centres around a crime which is committed by a male character who is being manipulated by a female character.

■ *e.g.* *Double Indemnity* (Billy Wilder, 1944), *The Big Sleep* (Howard Hawks, 1946)

filmography: a list of the films made by a particular director, often arranged in chronological order.

film school: an institution which specialises in the teaching of all aspects of film-making.

■ *e.g.* the New York Film School, whose alumni include *Martin Scorsese*

film stock: film which has not yet been exposed or used to shoot images.

filter: a piece of plastic or a gel which is placed over the *lens* of a *camera* in order to create a *specific effect*.

■ *e.g.* Colour filters can be placed over a film lens to create a sense of mood or atmosphere.

final cut: the final version of a film after the *editing* stage has been completed and the *sound track* has been attached.

■ Some directors have control of the final cut and oversee the very last stages of the film-making process. Conversely, studios may have the right to the final cut and may change a film to fit their own criteria.

Fincher, David (1962–): film *director*.

■ Born in Denver, USA, Fincher began his film career as an optical *special effects* director on films such as *Indiana Jones and the Temple of Doom* (*Steven Spielberg*, 1984) and *The Never Ending Story* (Wolfgang Petersen, 1984). He spent several years directing music videos (including some for Madonna) before graduating to film direction. Fincher commands huge budgets for his films, but is still able to inject his work with an original, and often dark, vision.

■ Filmography: *Alien 3* (1992), *Se7en* (1995), *The Game* (1997), *Fight Club* (1999), *Panic Room* (2001)

fish-eye lens: a type of camera *lens* with a scope of nearly 180 degrees.

■ The middle of a shot taken with a fish-eye lens is more prominent than the edges, which can create a distorted viewpoint. Fish-eye lenses are often used to generate a sense of disorientation for the audience.

flashback: a scene or moment in which the story of a film jumps backwards in time.

■ Flashbacks may be used to show past events or to explain a character's state of mind or motivations. See also *flash forward*.

■ *e.g.* At the end of Hitchcock's 1956 film *Marnie* there is a flashback to the main character's past which explains her state of mind.

flash forward: a scene or moment in which the story of a film jumps ahead to the future.

■ Flash forwards do not represent events which have already happened (see *flashback*), but tend to be used to indicate a character's fears for the future.

■ *e.g.* Donald Sutherland's character in Nicolas Roeg's 1973 film, *Don't Look Now*, experiences a flash forward which presents him with his own death.

flicks: a slang term for film or cinema.

■ The term originated from a description of early black and white cinema, which flickered due to slow projection speed. The expression 'going to the flicks' was common in the mid-twentieth century but has fallen out of use.

fly-on-the-wall: a style of documentary film-making which attempts to present events as if they have not been influenced by the presence of a camera.

focus: the sharpness or otherwise of an image.

■ Sharp or clear focus allows the viewer to see everything on the screen plainly. Soft or blurred focus makes it difficult for the viewer to discern what is depicted. Blurred focus can be used deliberately by the film-maker in order to create a disorientating effect.

footage: the total amount of film shot over a particular period.

■ The term is derived from the original way of measuring film, in feet.

found footage: describes real images of events which are inserted into a fictional film.

■ Found footage can be used to create a reality effect within a film's story, as it will appear that the film is dealing with a situation which has a basis in real events.

■ *e.g.* Alain Resnais's 1955 film *Night and Fog*, about the Nazi concentration camps, included real footage of corpses, shot at actual concentration camps as they were being liberated at the end of the Second World War. Scenes which included images of decapitated bodies and emaciated corpses were cut before the film was released. The censors decided that these images were too horrific for the viewing public.

framing: the selection of elements such as *characters*, *setting* and *iconography* which make up a film frame.

■ The composition of a frame is important in the generation of meaning within a film. The director may decide to foreground a particular character, indicating dominance, or to empty the frame around a particular character, suggesting isolation. Objects may take on significance because of their positioning within the frame.

■ *e.g.* The scenes of Jewish people on the trains to Auschwitz in *Steven Spielberg*'s *Schindler's List* (1993) feature crammed frames with virtually no empty space, evoking the sense of confinement and claustrophobia which the prisoners are experiencing.

■ *TIP* The easiest way to evaluate framing is to *freeze frame* a film and study the elements which you can see on the screen at a given moment.

freeze frame: the effect of seemingly stopping a film in order to focus on one tiny section within it.

■ The film has not actually been stopped, but the frame which is focused on is repeated in order to generate the effect of frozen time. Freeze frames can be used by a director to pinpoint a significant moment within a film's story or to leave the viewers with a particular moment frozen in their minds at the end of a film.

French New Wave: the period within French film-making (late 1950s to early 1960s) in which directors such as François Truffaut and Jean-Luc Godard were making films with a different style and look from what had gone before.

■ These films were characterised by amoral heroes, experimental camera techniques and *narratives* which did not necessarily achieve *closure*. The French New Wave also had its own body of film writing, specifically that which was published in the magazine *Cahiers du Cinèma*. Directors such as Truffaut and Godard expounded their ideas for a new type of modern cinema in essays, which in turn influenced other young French film-makers of this period.

gaffer: the member of the film *crew* who is the chief technician or lighting technician.

■ The gaffer is responsible for lighting the set from instructions issued by the *cinematographer*. He/she instructs the crew where to place lights before and during filming.

gangster film: a type of film which focuses on a group of criminals.

■ Often the story within a gangster film begins with the success and increase in power and fortune of the criminals, but ends with their decline and fall. The stories in gangster films are violent and dramatic, and often focus on deteriorating relationships within criminal families or groups or the corrupting influence of power on one particular criminal.

■ *e.g.* Howard Hawk's 1932 film *Scarface*, Arthur Penn's 1967 film *Bonnie and Clyde*, **Francis Ford Coppola**'s *Godfather* trilogy and **Martin Scorsese**'s 1990 film *Goodfellas* all trace the rise and fall of a criminal protagonist.

gender: describes the sex of an individual and how their male or femaleness is constructed.

■ Unlike sex, which is biologically determined, an individual's gender is created through ideology. The study of gender within cinema concentrates on how men and women are presented to and understood by the audience. The expectations a viewer has of the *representation* of a particular gender will affect how that individual 'reads' a film. Critics look at whether gender representations resort to *stereotype* and consider how time and social attitudes affect the representations of men and women on the screen.

genre: the system of classifying films into categories or types including *horror films, musicals, thrillers, science fiction films* and *Westerns*.

■ 'Genre' is a French word which literally means 'kind'. Films within specific genres utilise similar *conventions* regarding characters, story types, settings, costumes, props and themes. Individual films within a particular genre may use conventions in an unusual way, but there are certain elements in most genres that are always present: Westerns always include cowboys, sheriffs, saloons and saloon girls, for example, and horror films always include frightening places, killers and victims.

■ Often a main genre can be subdivided into smaller *sub-genres*. Sub-genres of horror films, for example, include *vampire movies*, *slasher movies* and demonic possession films. Comedies can be *romantic*, *slapstick* and *screwball*.

■ *TIP* Don't forget that a film may mix genres and become a hybrid form. A film could be classified as science fiction/horror, for example, or comedy/ Western.

Gilliam, Terry (1940–): film director.

■ Born in Minneapolis, after moving to London Gilliam began working for the BBC. He then joined John Cleese, Michael Palin et al. to become part of the television series *Monty Python and the Flying Circus* (1969–76). This surreal and zany series influenced Gilliam in his future film-making.

■ Filmography: *Monty Python and the Holy Grail* (1975), *Jabberwocky* (1977), *Time Bandits* (1981), *The Adventures of Baron Munchausen* (1989), *The Fisher King* (1991), *Twelve Monkeys* (1995), *Fear and Loathing in Las Vegas* (1998)

golden age of Hollywood: the *Hollywood studio system* had its golden age between 1930 and 1948.

■ During this period, film *production* was on a 'production-line model', often criticised for resulting in films that were formulaic and too similar. Five companies dominated the film industry at this time, each controlled by a powerful individual, a *mogul*, who oversaw all aspects of the studio's functioning. Darryl F. Zanuck was one of the most famous and controlled the careers of many important *stars*. Betty Grable, a huge star during the Hollywood golden age, was one of Zanuck's most famous products.

Gothic horror film: a horror film which draws its story from works of Gothic fiction such as Bram Stoker's *Dracula* (1897) and Mary Shelley's *Frankenstein* (1818).

■ Gothic horror films use the monsters featured in these stories, such as vampires, werewolves and mummies.

■ *e.g.* Films, such as *The Curse of Frankenstein* (Terence Fisher, 1957) and *Dracula Prince of Darkness* (Terence Fisher, 1966), produced by the Hammer studios from the 1950s to the 1970s, which often starred Christopher Lee or Vincent Price, drew heavily on Gothic fiction.

graphic match: an *editing* effect in which two different objects of the same shape *dissolve* from one into the other.

■ A graphic match is often used in order to promote the idea of a connection between the two images.

g

■ *e.g.* At the end of the famous shower scene in Hitchcock's *Psycho* (1960), a graphic match links the image of the water swirling down the plug hole and the eye of the victim, Marion Crane. The linking of these two circular images not only matches the draining water with the draining life of Marion, but generates a feeling of spiralling into something horrific.

grip: a person who works on a film *set* and is responsible for setting up equipment and scenery.
■ A grip helps to move sets and sets up *lighting* devices and *camera* mounts.

gross: the amount of money a film makes before expenses for publicity and advertising have been deducted.
■ The gross for a film may be a massive sum, but nowadays the P&A (publicity and advertising) budgets for films are huge and can severely reduce eventual profits.

Hammer: a British film studio most famous for the production of *horror films* in the 1950s, 1960s and 1970s.

■ Hammer horror films are characterised by their *Gothic* environments and storylines. The over-the-top acting styles, stereotypical Gothic castles, wilting heroines and evil monsters offered a contrast to the bleak, realistic environments and social issues presented in other British films during the same period. Peter Cushing and Christopher Lee acted in many of the most famous examples of Hammer horror films.

■ *e.g. The Curse of Frankenstein* (Terence Fisher, 1957), *Dracula* (Terence Fisher, 1958)

hand-held camera: a portable *camera*.

■ Hand-held cameras are often used to approximate the viewpoint of a character while they are moving. The slight jerkiness can be used to resemble a character's viewpoint.

■ *e.g. The Blair Witch Project* (Daniel Myrick, 1999) was shot entirely using hand-held cameras, as if the characters themselves were shooting the footage. In this way, the viewer sees the same disorientating, chilling images as the characters lost in the woods.

Hays Office: the name given to the Motion Picture Producers and Distributors of America, after its president William H. Hays.

■ The Hays Office was founded in 1922 to monitor and censor films. It established the Motion Picture Production Code in 1930 for the purposes of reducing the sexual content of films.

hegemony: the process by which a dominant idea (*ideology*) is maintained.

■ Hegemony is initially created by powerful institutions such as the government, the mass media, religion or the family. The ideas which come from these institutions become powerful and dominant in their turn.

h

heritage film: a phrase used to describe a type of film which draws its subject matter from either a classic work of literature or a significant historical event.
- Heritage films use authentic costumes and locations in order to dramatise a novel or a historical figure's life.
- *e.g.* *Sense and Sensibility* (*Ang Lee*, 1995), *Elizabeth* (Shekhar Kapur, 1998)
- *TIP* Heritage films are often associated with British cinema. In terms of *marketing*, they transfer well to a US (or global) market, because they offer a view of British life and history which is recognisable to other cultures.

high-angle shot: a shot that places the camera above eye level, looking down on characters or action. What the audience views therefore seems vulnerable or insignificant.

high concept: describes big-budget films which incorporate dramatic action sequences and sophisticated *special effects*.
- The term is often associated with *Hollywood* films, which have huge *marketing* budgets and are aimed at a wide, *mainstream* audience.
- *e.g.* *Terminator 2* (*James Cameron*, 1991), *The Matrix* (the Wachowski Brothers, 1999)

high-key lighting: a type of *lighting* which illuminates a scene evenly and emphasises bright colours.
- Often used in comedies or musicals to create a happy, positive atmosphere within a scene.

Hollywood: area of Los Angeles, California, famous for film production.
- The Hollywood studio system had its *golden age* between 1930 and 1948. After the Second World War a combination of social, economic and political forces reduced the dominance of the five major Hollywood companies and brought the *studio system* to an end. After years of financial hardship and anxiety resulting from the war, many Americans moved to the suburbs in an attempt to create stress-free family lives. This movement of the population out of the cities led to a decline in cinema attendance and box-office takings. Eventually, many of the big movie palaces were forced to close. The end to the studio system came in 1948, with the 'Paramount Decree', a Supreme Court ruling which forced the major companies to sell their cinemas. Effectively, the monopoly of the Big Five was broken (although four of them still exist).
- The Hollywood of today is a different place. There are more than a dozen studios in Los Angeles, including MGM, Warner Bros, Sony Pictures Studios, Paramount, Universal, Twentieth Century Fox and Dreamworks, but studios no longer make films; they make film deals.

homage: a respectful reference within a film to another film or director, or the affectionate replication of a film style. See also *intertextuality*.

■ A homage occurs when a director decides to use a style, images or references from a previous film in order to acknowledge the impact of that film or its director.

■ *e.g.* Todd Haynes's film *Far from Heaven* (2003) uses heightened colours, suburban settings and discussions of middle America in the 1950s in a direct homage to the 1950s films of director Douglas Sirk.

horror film: a type of film which aims to terrify the viewer.

■ Horror films use the supernatural, the unknown or graphic depictions of violence to generate fear in the audience. They tend to include predictable elements, such as frightening places, monstrous characters, eerie or disturbing lighting and a diminishing group of victims.

■ *e.g.* F. W. Murnau's *Nosferatu* (1922) was one of the first cinematic examples of the horror genre. Since the 1920s, horror films have been a constant form of cinema production, and many different variations have developed. *Rosemary's Baby*, Roman Polanski's 1968 film concerning a demonic cult, and William Friedkin's 1973 film *The Exorcist*, which told the story of a young girl possessed by demonic forces, both used the idea of possession to frighten viewers. *David Cronenberg*'s horror films, such as *Rabid* (1976), *The Brood* (1979) and *The Fly* (1986), are examples of horror films which used the invasion of the body to frighten the viewer. *The Texas Chainsaw Massacre* (Tobe Hooper, 1974) and *The Hills Have Eyes* (Wes Craven, 1977) used humans with monstrous potential to generate fear. From Gothic creatures, such as vampires and werewolves, to the devil, parasites and psychotic individuals, horror films have employed a variety of terrifying 'monsters'.

hype: the excitement generated about a forthcoming film release.

■ Hype is used by the company responsible for *marketing* a film to create public interest in a forthcoming release. It may take the form of press articles, poster and trailer campaigns or word of mouth. The greater the hype surrounding a film, the greater potential there is for *box-office* success.

hypodermic model: a theory of audience response in which the viewer is passive and absorbs the messages offered by a film without challenging them.

■ The word 'hypodermic' implies that meaning is injected directly into the viewer.

iconography: the objects or images in a film which have a potential meaning beyond the literal or obvious.

■ The study of iconography is the process of analysing objects, costumes and other images in order to discover what they might mean. Their meanings may be affected by the era in which the film is set, its social or political context and the attitudes which are current at the time when the film is being watched.

identification: a viewer's sense of sharing attributes, feelings or experiences with a character in a film or of having an interest in the issue addressed by the film.

■ Identification allows the viewer to become involved with a character's life or an issue being discussed. It is a means by which the film-maker can engage the audience's deep attention.

ideology: a system of ideas, values and beliefs which are held as important by a group or society in general.

■ Ideology describes a set of shared beliefs, which can include attitudes to class, race, sexual orientation and gender. A dominant ideology is a set of ideas held by the majority. It can affect the way an individual responds to a film or the types of story, character and images seen within a film. If the dominant ideology at a particular point in history were that women were inferior to men, an ideological study of the films produced at that time would show whether this dominant social attitude had influenced the work of film-makers.

IMAX: a type of film production and projection which creates huge screen images for the viewer (an example of *big-screen cinema*).

■ For the film consumer, IMAX is very different from the standard filmgoing experience. Usually the films available in the IMAX format are non-narrative; they offer an experience (of being under the sea, in space, on the moon etc.) or are a showpiece for technology (3D films and animated spectacles). The IMAX film experience is one of immersion. It offers huge, digital, *surround-sound* systems and images which enter the front and peripheral (side) vision, creating a total physical viewing experience.

■ The film used in IMAX cameras is 70 mm, as opposed to the standard 35 mm. The projector for an IMAX screen is the size of a small car and the screen is four to five times the height of a double-decker bus.

independent cinema: describes films which have not been produced by one of the major *Hollywood* studios or with major studio backing.

■ *e.g.* Directors *David Lynch, Spike Lee* and Jim Jarmusch are particularly associated with independent film-making, as they do not work for major studios.

insert shot: a shot inserted into a sequence to give extra information to the viewer.

■ An insert shot differs from the main shot of a sequence by taking a different view and giving more specific information.

■ *e.g.* If the main shot is of a character looking in at a shop window, the insert shot might show what the character is looking at.

institutions: the people who have a role in producing film texts, the companies or organisations they represent and the processes of *production, distribution* and *marketing* in which both are involved.

■ Film institutions include studios, distributors, exhibitors and classification bodies, and, at an individual level, directors, editors, producers and screen writers.

■ *e.g. MGM, AOL/TimeWarner, Disney*, the *British Board of Film Classification*

interior monologue: a passage of 'speech' by one character, which none of the other characters can hear.

■ Interior monologues are often used as a means of giving the viewer, but not the other characters, information about a character's state of mind. It is as if the viewer were hearing the thoughts of the character.

internet: a global computer network which provides access to roughly a billion pages of information on the World Wide Web.

■ For the film industry, the internet has become central to the *marketing* of films. Any *mainstream* film advertised at the cinema is guaranteed to have its own website. Many smaller, more independent films also have their own sites.

■ Before a film is released, its website will include information on the cast, the film-makers and the film itself. The site may provide a *synopsis* of the plot, plus *trailers* and *clips* from the film. For fans or potential viewers, the site provides pre-release information from which they can make a judgement on whether or not to see a film. Discussion boards on a website can make the potential viewer of a film feel part of its 'viewing community'.

■ For the film distributor in charge of marketing a film, there are numerous advantages to a website. In comparison to a poster campaign, cinema trailers or press advertising, a website is relatively cheap and those which also sell merchandise can be almost self-financing. A website can be continually updated too to take account of any new or amended information.

■ Official websites provide an important marketing tool for the distributor, but unofficial sites have a slightly different function. These are apparently unconnected with the film-makers and provide a forum for fan reviews, gossip and unauthorised information. Positive word of mouth is extremely important for a film's *box-office* success and unofficial sites are a useful indication of the pre-release response.

■ The internet can also provide a relatively inexpensive forum for the marketing of lower-budget films. Independent film-makers who have produced a film using digital cameras and editing programmes can create their own website and upload promotional images, clips and details. In this way, internet users can be targeted without the enormous marketing budgets available to major distribution companies.

■ *e.g. The Blair Witch Project* (Daniel Myrick, 1999) is a perfect example of a lower-budget film which used the internet very successfully prior to release. The internet *teaser* campaign for the film, which posted information about a seemingly real event, inspired the kind of word of mouth which is invaluable for a film's marketing campaign and eventual box-office success.

intertextuality: the process by which one film refers either explicitly or implicitly to another. See also *homage.*

■ A character in a film might discuss another film explicitly or a film might use music, sets, objects or images which are deliberately similar to another film. Intertextuality is used to generate meaning for the viewer. It can be used to give information about characters, issues and even the influences on a director's style.

■ *e.g. David Lynch*'s film *Wild at Heart* (1990) uses many images from the film *The Wizard of Oz* (1939), including a nightmare sequence in which the character Lula's mother is seen on a broomstick, dressed as the Wicked Witch of the West. Lula's fear of her mother's darker side is made more understandable by the intertextual reference.

intertitle: printed words which appear within a film, not as part of the title sequences.

■ Intertitles were used extensively in silent films in order to give the viewer information about what characters were saying.

jump cut: a type of *editing* which breaks the continuity of the viewing experience.

■ A jump cut jolts the viewer from one image or scene to another in a way which is disorientating and disrupts the *realism* of the film. Some directors use jump cuts to mark a stylistic difference between their films and more predictable *mainstream* films. Jump cuts are also used to indicate disorientation on the part of a character.

■ *e.g.* The *French New Wave* film-makers, who attempted to produce films which were different from the Hollywood mainstream, employed jump cuts to signal their films' difference.

juxtaposition: the placement of two images or *scenes* on either side of an edit for specific effect.

■ A director can build subtle connections between characters and places by using juxtaposed images.

■ *e.g.* If the scene of a crime were juxtaposed with a scene involving a particular character, the viewer might be encouraged to 'read' the character either as the criminal or as the investigator of the crime.

key light: the brightest light used within a *scene*.

■ The key light is used to light the whole scene, but may then be softened by other types of light to give a more naturalistic feel to the scene.

kung-fu film: a film in which the characters are competent in the martial art of kung-fu.

■ Kung-fu films include elaborately *choreographed* fight scenes and generally include a narrative in which a lone character is fighting, against the odds, to rescue somebody or prove something to him/herself.

■ *e.g.* *Fist of Fury* (Lo Wei, 1972) starring Bruce Lee

Lee, Ang (1954–): film director.
- Born in Taiwan, Lee was educated in the USA, studying film at the University of Illinois and New York University. He still retains close ties with Taiwan either through the thematic content, setting and characters of his films (*Pushing Hands, The Wedding Banquet, Eat Drink Man Woman*) or through directing US/Taiwanese co-productions (the previous three examples, plus *Crouching Tiger, Hidden Dragon*).
- Filmography: *Pushing Hands* (1992), *The Wedding Banquet* (1993), *Eat Drink Man Woman* (1994), *Sense and Sensibility* (1995), *The Ice Storm* (1997), *Ride with the Devil* (1999), *Crouching Tiger, Hidden Dragon* (2000)

Lee, Spike (1957–): film *director*.
- Born in Atlanta, USA, Lee spent most of his formative years in New York, which provides the setting for many of his films. He studied film at New York University before becoming a film director. Often hailed as one of the most successful examples of African-American film-makers, Lee is best known for films which directly address racial tensions.
- Filmography: *She's Gotta Have It* (1986), *School Daze* (1988), *Do the Right Thing* (1989), *Mo' Better Blues* (1990), *Jungle Fever* (1991), *Malcolm X* (1992), *Crooklyn* (1994), *Clockers* (1995), *Get on the Bus* (1996), *Girl 6* (1996), *Four Little Girls* (1997), *He Got Game* (1998), *Summer of Sam* (1999), *Bamboozled* (2000), *25th Hour* (2002).

lens: the part of a *camera* through which the images being shot are viewed.

lighting: the lights used within a scene which are essential in conveying the mood or atmosphere of a scene.
- The viewer can be drawn to objects or characters which are brightly lit or can be made nervous by shadows and obscured parts of the film frame.

linear narrative: a style of storytelling in which events happen chronologically and are felt to move forward in time.

■ Most films are structured using linear narratives. Events follow in a sequence and seem to be moving forward as if in real time. The *realism* that most films attempt to generate in order to maintain the continuous attention of the viewer is aided by linear narrative.

lip synching: the incorporation of speech into a film in such a way that the movements of the characters' lips fit what is being said.

■ If a dialogue is recorded again after filming has been completed, it has to be added to the film at the *postproduction* stage. If lip synching is not done accurately, the audience will be jolted out of its immersion in the film and there will be a comical effect of lips moving out of pace with the words heard.

■ Lip synching is important in the process of *dubbing*.

location: the place in which either a whole film or scenes from a film are shot.

■ Locations are real places which a film uses as environments for the story. The locations in a film are important in the generation of meaning. Locations can help the viewer to understand the characters' states of mind and social positions. They can also convey the *genre* of film being watched, e.g. an urban location would not be fitting for a traditional *Western*.

long shot: a shot in which the camera is distant from the character or object being photographed.

■ Long shots are often used to associate particular characters with particular environments and to evoke the relationship between character and environment. *Establishing shots* often take the form of long shots.

■ *e.g.* The opening sequence of the *Coen Brothers*' film *Fargo* (1996) used long shots of a snow-bound environment and a barely visible car driving up an otherwise empty road. The isolation of the characters in these harsh surroundings is evident from the beginning of the film.

lot: the area of land where a studio is located. It includes the offices, stages, dressing rooms and any other facilities needed for film production.

low-angle shot: a shot that positions the camera below eye level, looking up at a character, object or the action in a scene.

■ This type of shot tends to make what is shot look powerful, even threatening. See *high-angle shot*.

■ *e.g.* At the beginning of *James Cameron*'s *Titanic* (1997), the low-angle shot of the vessel exaggerates its awesome size and makes its subsequent sinking even more spectacularly shocking.

low-budget film: a film which is made with very little financial backing.

■ During the Hollywood *golden age* (1930–48) when the *studio system* prevailed it also indicated a lower-quality film which would have been shown alongside the main feature in a *double bill.*

low-key lighting: a type of lighting which creates a dim or underlit scene.
- The overall appearance of the scene is shadowy and ominous. Low-key lighting is often used in *film noir, horror films* and *thrillers.*

Lynch, David (1946–): film *director.*
- Born in Montana, USA, Lynch studied fine art before becoming a film director and still exhibits his artwork today. He is perhaps most famous for the surreal, ominous and disturbing worlds which he creates in his films and for his particular way of uncovering the strange underbelly of American society. He retains a great degree of control over his films and is famous not only for his cinematic vision, but for his attention to detail during the film-making process.
- Filmography: *Eraserhead* (1976), *The Elephant Man* (1980), *Dune* (1984), *Blue Velvet* (1986), *Twin Peaks* (television series, 1989–91), *Wild at Heart* (1990), *Twin Peaks: Fire Walk with Me* (1992), *Lost Highway* (1997), *The Straight Story* (1999), *Mulholland Drive* (2001)

MacGuffin: a term coined by Alfred Hitchcock to describe an element of a film plot which seems to be significant, but is eventually revealed to have no significance at all.

■ *e.g.* *Quentin Tarantino*'s film *Pulp Fiction* (1994) includes two characters who are guarding a briefcase. The contents of the briefcase are treated with the utmost respect by those guarding it, but the audience never finds out what the contents are and comes to realise that they have no real significance in terms of the plot.

macro analysis: a phrase used in film studies to describe the kind of analysis which concentrates on *narrative* and *genre*.

■ Narrative and genre cannot be 'seen' within a film in the same way as, for example, *mise-en-scène*. However, the choices which a film-maker makes regarding narrative and genre elements are equally important in the construction of meaning. See also *micro analysis*.

mainstream cinema: a term used to describe films which are made for a wide audience.

■ Mainstream films tend to use universal storylines and recognisable actors and do not generally employ experimental camerawork or editing. These films usually have a higher budget than *independent* films and are more likely to be shown in a large *multiplex* type of cinema. Mainstream films are created for entertainment and profit, not to make a social, political or artistic point.

■ *e.g.* Sam Raimi's *Spiderman* (2002), Peter Jackson's *Lord of the Rings* films (2001, 2002 and 2003)

make-up: the cosmetics used on actors during filming.

■ Make-up is an essential tool for all film actors, but it can also be used to generate particular meanings.

■ *e.g.* Tom Hanks's make-up in the film *Philadelphia* (Jonathon Demme, 1993) allows viewers to see the physical ravages of AIDS and adds to their identification with, and empathy for, his plight. Subtle differences in the use of make-

m

up can also indicate historical period. The 1960s scenes in the Austin Powers films, for example, are given more realism by the actors' use of the heavy eyeliner and bright lipstick of that period.

marketing: the process by which information about a forthcoming film is delivered to the potential *audience*, in order to try to ensure the film's (*box-office* or critical) success.

■ Many different strategies are used in the marketing of a film. Advertising is perhaps the most obvious and includes posters and *trailers*. Press articles (known as press releases) in which information about a film is supplied to the press by the film-makers are another form of marketing. Television interviews with stars also provide exposure for a film and are an effective marketing tool.

masala movie: a term used to describe the films produced in Hindi for mainstream Indian cinema.

■ Masala movies are recognisable as they mix different styles of film in a way that might appear strange to a western viewer. A masala movie may include elements of action, melodrama and comedy.

■ Most *Bollywood* products are masala movies. They mix many genres to reach the widest possible audience.

master shot: a shot that includes all of the action in one particular sequence.

■ At the *editing* stage, any *close-ups* on characters or *medium close-ups* of conversations can be inserted into the master shot. The master shot acts as a constant background of action which is then punctuated with other shots.

mediation: the process by which the viewer's own experiences are brought to the viewing process and combine with the messages in a film to generate an individual response.

■ The term is often used with reference to passive and active viewing. Passive viewers do not question what they see or challenge the messages of the film (see *hypodermic model*). Active viewers are more likely to 'mediate' their viewing by bringing their own attitudes and opinions into the viewing process.

medium close-up: a shot that gives a chest-up view of individual characters.

■ Medium close-ups are often used to shoot two characters in conversation.

medium shot: a shot that takes the body of a character from the knees up.

■ Medium shots are often used to shoot groups of people talking.

melodrama: a type of film which involves family or relationship tensions and deliberately sets out to create emotional, often tearful, moments.

■ Melodramas present dramatic or traumatic events and are often aimed at a female audience, supposedly easily moved to tears.

■ *e.g.* *Mildred Pierce* (Michael Curtiz, 1945), *Steel Magnolias* (Herbert Ross, 1989)

m

merchandising: the sale of products associated with a particular film release.

■ The merchandise for a film can generate huge amounts of revenue and provide an effective further means of advertising. The sale of toys, games, clothes etc. can prove more profitable than *box-office* takings. Actors sometimes demand a percentage of merchandising sales as part of their fee.

method acting: a style of acting (originating in the *Actor's Studio*) in which the actor attempts to create the character psychologically, as well as physically.

■ Method actors attempt to embody or become the character they are playing and create a complete psychological *back story* for their character in order to attempt to make him or her more real for the audience.

■ *e.g.* Robert DeNiro went to great lengths to 'live' the character of Jake La Motta, who he played in Martin Scorsese's *Raging Bull* (1980). Rather than wear padding for the period when the boxer had given up his sport and had 'run to fat', DeNiro actually gained the necessary amount of weight.

MGM (Metro-Goldwyn-Mayer): one of the five major *Hollywood* studios during the *golden age* of the Hollywood *studio system* (1930–48).

■ MGM was perhaps the most famous of the major studios. Marcus Loew bought Metro Pictures Corporation in 1920 and Goldwyn Pictures in 1924. In the late 1920s he merged with Louis B. Mayer's production company to form MGM. Its *stars* included Greta Garbo, Clark Gable and Judy Garland. Mayer was the head of the studio (*mogul*).

micro analysis: the study of the technical details of a film, i.e. *cinematography*, *mise-en-scène* and *sound*.

■ Micro elements are the parts of a film which help create its look, narrative, characters, settings and meanings. The director's choice of camerawork, editing, sound and mise-en-scène provides the often invisible elements which create what you eventually see on the screen. Micro elements are important not only as building blocks for how a film appears to its audience, but as ways of communicating different meanings.

■ Micro elements can be used in a way the audience expects, thus providing a predictable viewing experience, or they can be used in an unusual way to make viewers think and challenge their expectations of a film.

■ *TIP* Make sure that in your essays, you not only identify and describe the micro elements you have chosen, but also discuss how they are used and what the effect of this use is on the viewer.

■ *e.g.* Imagine the kind of music that might be associated with the villain of a film. Your expectations are probably of an ominous, dark, brooding piece. If your expectations were met, it would be clear how you were supposed to respond to that character, but if the music were lighter or sadder, rather than chilling, then you might have to revise your estimation.

mise-en-scène: a French term which literally means 'put into the frame', this describes everything which can be seen by the viewer in a single frame of a film.

■ An analysis of mise-en-scène will include all details of *set, location, props, costumes, make-up*, use of *colour* and actors' movements which can be seen in one particular frame of a film. The director's choice of *mise-en-scène* elements is crucial in the generation of meaning. Information concerning mood, atmosphere, characters' states of mind and emotions can all be generated through *mise-en-scène*.

■ *e.g.* The character Lester Burnham in Sam Mendes's film *American Beauty* (1999) works in a grey and beige office space, in which he occupies a tiny cramped cubicle. His feeling of entrapment, depression and disillusionment is effectively created by the set and the props used.

mogul: describes the powerful individuals who ran studios during the *golden age* of the *Hollywood studio system* (1930–48).

■ *e.g.* Darryl F. Zanuck was one of the most famous of the cinema moguls and controlled the career of many stars. Betty Grable, a huge star during the Hollywood golden age, was one of Zanuck's most famous products.

montage editing: the process by which dramatic images are placed next to one another in order to suggest a certain idea.

■ 'Montage' is taken from French, and means 'assembly'.

■ The term is often used to suggest *editing* which creates disorientating sequences that break with usual narrative conventions of chronological time. See also *continuity editing*.

■ *e.g.* One of the first examples of montage editing appears in Sergei Eisenstein's 1925 film *Battleship Potemkin*. The images of the innocent victims being killed by troops during the famous Odessa Steps sequence are shown rapidly and intercut with images of the troops. This sequence, which does not attempt to move the narrative or the time structure of the film forward, gives a clear indication to the audience that the state's attitude to the people is oppressive and indiscriminate.

multiplex: a type of cinema complex which has a large number of screens.

■ Multiplex cinemas first appeared in the 1980s and are designed to show a large number of films to large audiences. The majority of films shown at multiplexes are *mainstream* with certificates (such as U, PG, 12 and 15) which have the potential to attract the largest audiences.

musical: a type of film in which characters perform songs as part of the narrative.

■ Musicals often have a romance at the centre of their plots and include song and dance routines.

■ *e.g. West Side Story* (Robert Wise, 1961), *Moulin Rouge* (Baz Luhrmann, 2001)

m

myth: a story, usually derived from Greek mythology, which can be used as a basic structure for a film's narrative.

■ *e.g.* The myth of Orpheus, who descended into the underworld in order to save his love, Euridice, provides the basis of many plots in which a character faces adversity in order to try to save his/her lover. For example, in Vincent Ward's 1998 film *What Dreams May Come* Robin Williams has to save his wife from hell.

narrative: describes the structure and movement of a story in a film.

national cinema: the films produced within a particular country.
- The national cinema for any one country can be difficult to define. Whether the criteria for identifying films as examples of a national cinema are based on location, cast, crew, characterisation, funding or themes is a much-debated question.
- *e.g.* British film is a case in point. Recent British film products have included those which deal with the issue of other ethnic groups living in Britain (*Bend it Like Beckham*, Gurinda Chadha, 2002, *East is East*, Ayub Khan-Din, 1999, *Bhaji on the Beach* , Gurinda Chadha, 1993); films which have American stars (*Four Weddings and a Funeral*, Mike Newell, 1994, *Sliding Doors*, Peter Howitt, 1998); low-budget films which are targeted at a British audience (Shane Meadows's *A Room for Romeo Brass*, 1999 and *24/7*, 1997); and those which have gained success and subsequent financing from a US market (*The Full Monty*, Peter Cattaneo, 1997, *Trainspotting*, Danny Boyle, 1996, *Billy Elliot*, Stephen Daldry, 2000). All of these films have elements of Britishness about them, but are such a diverse group as to make a clear definition of British national cinema extremely difficult.

New Wave: a period in a nation's film-making history in which new ideas are in evidence.
- New Wave films are often characterised by innovations in style, narrative and characterisation.
- *e.g.* The films of *French New Wave* directors, such as François Truffaut and Jean-Luc Godard, often used amoral heroes, fragmented storylines and experimental *camera movement* in order to signal their difference from *mainstream* cinema.

non-diegetic sound: sound which does not exist within the story of a film, but is put onto the film in *postproduction*.

n

■ This type of sound could be in the form of a music *sound track,* a *voice-over* or extra sounds which enhance the meaning of elements within the film.

■ *e.g.* Bernard Herrmann's haunting sound track for *Martin Scorsese*'s film *Taxi Driver* (1975) and the shrill and repetitive violin sounds which he created as the sound track for the shower scene in Hitchcock's *Psycho* (1960)

Obscene Publications Act (1959 and 1964): government legislation relating to the publishing or broadcasting of materials deemed to deprave or corrupt.

■ The Obscene Publications Act outlined criteria which could be used to assess film content. If a film is deemed to 'deprave or corrupt' those who might see it, then a prosecution under the Obscene Publications Act may be brought against the film-makers. No film has yet been successfully prosecuted under this act.

oedipal trajectory: a term derived from psychoanalysis, used to describe a type of narrative seen in *mainstream cinema*. The name comes from plays written in the fifth century BC by Sophocles which tell the story of Oedipus, who kills a king and marries the queen, only to discover that the king was his father and the queen his mother. The trials and challenges faced by Oedipus are the events translated into film narratives.

■ A storyline concerning a male character who has to contend with challenging circumstances, but eventually succeeds in overcoming hurdles and restoring order, would be considered to have an oedipal trajectory.

180 degree rule: a rule which keeps the position of the camera on the same side of the frame on either side of an edit.

■ An imaginary line is drawn across what is seen in an individual frame. If the camera is on one side of the frame in one shot, then in the next shot it remains on that side. If the camera were shifted from one side of the frame to another, the effect would be disorientating for the viewer. The 180 degree rule is adhered to in order to create an illusion of *realism* within a film. Most *mainstream* films adhere to the 180 degree rule in order to keep viewers' attention focused on the action, rather than jolting them into realising that they are watching a film and that camera set-ups are being used.

oppositional reading: a viewer's response to a film which challenges the meanings and messages offered by the film.

■ An oppositional reading will not passively accept the ideas or moral position indicated within a film, but will question what is being seen and offer a subjective conclusion.

Oscar: the statue which is presented to the winner of an American *Academy Award*.

■ Oscars were allegedly given their name because an early librarian of the academy, Margaret Herrick, said that the statue reminded her of her uncle Oscar.

out-take: a shot which is rejected at the *editing* stage and is not included in the final film.

overhead shot: a shot in which the *camera* is positioned above the character, action or object being filmed.

■ Overhead shots are often used in order to make characters look trapped in their environment or vulnerable to attack.

package: a combination of various elements of a film's production which are presented to potential financers.
- The producer might put together details of the *director, cast* and *crew* of a film, along with the writer and initial ideas for the film's script, in an attempt to sell the idea of the film more effectively.

panning: the horizontal movement of a *camera* from left to right or vice versa.
- The base of the camera is static within a panning shot. It is only the camera body which moves.
- Pans are used in many ways: to indicate a particular character's point of view on a scene, for example, or to introduce the viewer to a particular setting or piece of action.
- *TIP* Although both a pan and a *tracking shot* use a horizontal movement, in a tracking shot the base of the camera moves too.

parallel editing: a type of *editing* which allows two or more possibly connected stories in a film to run at the same time.
- Parallel editing is very common. By taking the viewer from one story to another and then back again, it allows a director to imply connections between simultaneous events.

Paramount: one of the five major *Hollywood* studios during the *golden age* of the *studio system* (1930–48).
- Paramount had more than 1,000 theatres in its cinema chain and therefore had the biggest hold over film showing.

parody: a comic imitation of another film.
- A parody uses all the ingredients of a particular style of film, but deploys those elements for humorous effect.
- *e.g.* Mel Brooks's parody of the *Western, Blazing Saddles* (1974)

pastiche: a film which borrows stylistic and narrative elements from other films, usually of the same type.

- A pastiche does not use elements of other films or film styles for a purely comic effect, but blends them into its own story.
- *e.g.* Quentin Tarantino's *Pulp Fiction* (1994) is a pastiche of American popular culture in the 1950s.

patriarchy: describes the dominant role of men within a state, organisation or group.
- In film studies, it is often applied to the film industry, especially in *Hollywood*, which has more male directors and studio executives than female and seems to offer film products which reflect this.

PG: a level of classification which indicates that children of any age can see a film but that parental guidance should be given about whether it is suitable for very young children.
- PG films should not include content which will disturb children of 8 years or over. A PG certificate guarantees a wide-ranging audience for a film, so producers often attempt to gain this certificate. The criteria against which the *British Board of Film Classification* assesses films for PG certification are:
  - More serious issues and themes can be discussed in a PG film than in a film with a U classification, e.g. crime, domestic violence and racism.
  - Only mild bad language is permissible.
  - Natural nudity is acceptable, providing there is no sexual connotation.
  - Mild sexual references and innuendo are allowed, but they have to be discreet and infrequent.
  - Moderate violence is allowed, as long as it is justified by its setting, e.g. within a historical context.
  - There can be no glamorisation of fighting or weapons.
  - Horror elements are allowed, but frightening sequences must not be overly long or intense.
  - No references may be made to illegal drugs or drug use.

pitch: a short description of a film, including brief details of characters and the main elements of the plot, which a writer might send to a producer.
- *e.g. The Player* (Robert Altman, 1992) includes a satirical scene in which an aspiring writer attempts to pitch a film to a studio executive. The executive gives him less than a minute to outline the main elements of character and plot.

plot: a term used to describe everything on the cinema screen which is used to give *narrative* information.
- The story of a film is the basic outline of events and characters. The plot includes those strategies, for example relating to sound or camera, which give the viewer information about the movement of time within the narrative and the motivations of the characters.

p

point-of-view shot (POV): a shot which shows the point of view of a character.
■ A point-of-view shot can encourage the audience to identify with a character or empathise with his/her situation. These shots can also be used to disorientate the viewer if they are not attributed to a particular character or if the point of view is from a character with bad motives.
■ *e.g.* The opening sequence in John Carpenter's film *Halloween* (1978) uses a point-of-view shot to position the viewers as if they were Michael Myers, who stabs his sister to death. Carpenter uses a point-of-view shot to force the viewer to watch the killing from a disturbingly close position.

polysemic: a term used to indicate that an aspect of a film (e.g. an image, an object or a sound) has a number of different meanings.
■ A polysemic image, object or sound can be read in a number of ways and the viewer is not confined to one interpretation.
■ *e.g.* The famous shot of the snowstorm ornament which is dropped by Kane at the beginning of Orson Welles's film *Citizen Kane* (1941) seems important within the plot of the film but has no single clear meaning; it is polysemic.

pornography: films which have extremely explicit sexual content and are sold purely to satisfy the potential viewer's sexual desires.
■ Pornographic films may have explicit heterosexual or homosexual content. They are the subject of much debate and nowadays are not given cinema release but move straight to video. Pornographic films can be described as either hard or soft core. Hard-core pornography includes shots of actual penetration and ejaculation, whereas soft-core pornography has sexual content, but is less explicit (see *sexploitation film*).

postmodernism: a body of theory which began in the 1960s and reached its height in the 1980s and 1990s.
■ In film studies, the term 'postmodernist' is often used to describe films which break with conventional narrative structures or reference other films, novels or pieces of artwork within their style or story.
■ *e.g.* Quentin Tarantino's films, such as *Reservoir Dogs* (1991), *Pulp Fiction* (1994) and *Jackie Brown* (1997), are often described as postmodernist because they use fragmented time within their narratives and are full of references to other film styles.

postproduction: the stage of film-making which comes after the main body of the filming has been done.
■ The postproduction stage includes *editing*, titling, the addition of a *sound track*, the inclusion of graphics and the incorporation of *special effects*. See also *preproduction*.

p

Potter, Sally (1949–): film *director*.

■ Born in the UK, Potter has also worked as a dancer, composer and choreographer and has used this experience in both the content and the production of her films. She is a leading British female director and has produced many films which articulate the female experience.

■ Filmography: *The Gold Diggers* (1983), *Orlando* (1992), *The Tango Lesson* (1997), *The Man who Cried* (2000)

POV: see *point-of-view shot.*

preferred reading: the meaning that a film-maker intends the audience to derive from a film.

■ If audiences accept the preferred reading of a film, they are agreeing with and not challenging the messages and values conveyed by the film. The advent of DVDs has given rise to an interesting debate concerning preferred readings. The director's commentary which is included on a DVD will offer the preferred reading, but some people believe that this unfairly influences viewers' interpretations. Although the director is creatively responsible for the film, his or her interpretation of the final film is just one reading.

premiere: the first showing of the *final cut* of a film.

■ Premieres are often high-profile events, attended by *stars* and other celebrities, and they provide film producers with valuable publicity.

preproduction: the period in the film-making process before filming begins, in which the producer of the film organises details of financing, *locations*, *cast* and *crew*. See also *postproduction*.

prequel: a film which tells the story leading up to a previously released film.

■ Prequels allow film-makers to capitalise on the success of one film by using many of the same elements (e.g. *characters*, *locations*, *special effects*) in another, connected film. See also *sequel*.

■ *e.g.* George Lucas's two *Star Wars* prequels, *The Phantom Menace* (1999) and *Attack of the Clones* (2002), allowed the producers to target existing *Star Wars* fans as well as a potential new market.

press kit: a package of materials supplied to magazine and newspaper journalists by the *distributor* of a film, which includes *stills*, video sequences, *cast* and *crew* biographies and a *plot* synopsis.

■ A press kit is intended to create a positive impression of a film in the minds of journalists and, via them, the viewing public.

preview: a showing of a film, usually to critics, before the main cinematic release.

■ Previews allow the producers of a film to gain critical feedback, usually in the form of press reviews.

producer: the individual who organises funding for a film and puts together details of the *locations, cast* and *crew*.

■ A film producer is responsible for the development of a script from an idea to the finished article. He/she is also responsible for any hiring or firing during the film's production.

production: a term used to describe the period of film-making in which the film is being shot.

production company: a company which has responsibility for the finances, *location, cast* and *crew* of a film.

■ Today many actors have formed their own production companies in order to have more control over films in which they appear or in which they have some other interest.

■ *e.g.* Liz Hurley and Hugh Grant have a production company called Simian Films. Jude Law, Sadie Frost, Sean Pertwee and Ewan McGregor are the actors behind Natural Nylon Films.

projection: the process of transmitting a film from celluloid or *digital* tape onto a cinema screen.

■ In the early days of cinema, projection was a complicated process, as two reels of film would be run simultaneously to avoid jumps in what was seen on the screen. The role of the projectionist was crucial in not only overseeing the smooth running of these two reels, but also changing reels in a way that did not halt projection. Today the system of projection for multiple films playing on different screens in large cinemas is often controlled through a central control panel.

promotional film: a film which aims to advertise a business, organisation or event.

prop: an object which is used on a film *set*.

■ The objects included in a scene are essential in the generation of meaning. They can give information about genre or historical period or character.

■ *e.g.* One of the ways in which it is possible to identify the *genre* of a film such as *The Matrix* (Wachowski Brothers, 1999) is through the props it uses. Space ships, futuristic weaponry and advanced computer systems all indicate that the genre of the film is science fiction. The puppets used by the central character in Spike Jonze's *Being John Malkovich* (1999) indicate a man whose dissatisfaction with his own life leads him to play out his fantasies through these wooden characters.

propaganda: the use of a medium, such as film, to promote the beliefs of a political party or the attitudes of a country or organisation.

p

■ Because films are a popular form of entertainment and are seen by a wide cross-section of the viewing public, they are a powerful medium for propaganda. A propaganda film may be fictional or seemingly real, but the point is to celebrate or promote a particular set of beliefs.

■ *e.g.* During the period of Nazi government in Germany many films were commissioned purely to promote Nazi ideology. The female director Leni Riefenstahl directed a number of propaganda films, such as *Triumph of the Will* (1935) and *Olympia* (1938), which documented Nazi successes.

Protection of Children Act 1978: government legislation which prohibits taking, distributing, possessing or advertising indecent images of children under 16 years old.

■ *e.g.* The film *Kids* (Larry Clark, 1995) came under investigation because it included images of a sexual and a sexually violent nature. The **British Board of Film Classification** was concerned that the film included images of a sexual nature involving children under the age of 16, but on investigation the cast were all found to be over the age of 16. Certain scenes were cut, including a rape scene in which an underage boy is seen sleeping in the foreground of the shot.

publicity still: a frozen moment from a film which might be sold or used for educational or marketing purposes. See also *action still*.

pyrotechnics: effects within a film which involve fire, fireworks or explosions.

■ These kinds of effects are often used during large-scale action sequences, where the visual spectacle of the scene is heightened by the use of fire or explosions.

■ *e.g.* There are numerous examples of films which have made full use of pyrotechnical effects in order to generate drama for the audience: *The Towering Inferno* (John Guillermin, 1974), *Armageddon* (Michael Bay, 1998) and *Star Wars* (George Lucas, 1977), to name just three.

■ *TIP* Remember that with the advent of *computer-generated imagery*, pyrotechnical effects can now be added to scenes in *postproduction*.

queer cinema: a term used to describe films which are made in order to portray or discuss some aspect of gay or lesbian experience.

■ The word 'queer', sometimes used as a term of abuse, is here attached positively to films which discuss issues concerning gays and lesbians.

■ *e.g. Desert Hearts* (Donna Deitch, 1985), which describes a lesbian relationship, and *The Living End* (Gregg Araki, 1992), which uses the format of a road movie to tell the story of two HIV-positive gay men

Rank Organisation: a British film company which was at its height in the 1940s.
■ Former owner of Pinewood Studios, Rank was once the largest backer and distributor of films in Britain and was behind some of the most significant films in British film history.
■ *e.g.* Powell and Pressburger's 1948 film *The Red Shoes* and the Laurence Olivier-directed *Henry V* (1944)

reaction shot: a shot which shows the reaction of a character either to an event or to another character.
■ Reaction shots are important to a film as they provide the viewer with information concerning the impact on characters of dialogue or events.

realism: describes the attempt to represent reality within a film.
■ Most films attempt to create some degree of realism in order to hold the attention of the audience. Viewers understand that what they are watching is a work of fiction, but look for elements which they can relate to as real in order to immerse themselves in the film's story (see also *identification*). Realism does not have to be seen explicitly in the objects, the look of characters or the plot of a film, but may exist more implicitly in the chronology, the issues dealt with or the motivations of a character.
■ Some films might use fragmented narratives or obvious camera techniques in order to break the viewer's sense of realism and discuss the act of film-making itself.
■ Films can be described as *social realist* if they are set within an environment which has not been glamorised and discuss social issues.
■ *e.g.* Lynne Ramsay's film *Ratcatcher* (1999) tells the story of a young boy who inadvertently lets his friend drown. The setting on a bleak council estate and the atmosphere of economic deprivation give this film a realist feel.

rear projection: see *back projection*.

rehearsal: a session in which actors practise their roles before filming.
■ Most *mainstream* films today include very little time for rehearsals, leaving it

up to the actors to try out various ways of presenting their characters in front of the camera. There are some directors, however, who have an enforced rehearsal time. The director Mike Leigh, for example, is famous for his 6–8-week rehearsal periods prior to shooting.

R18: a classification level which is specific to the assessment of videos depicting consenting sex between adults. These videos can only be supplied to adults through licensed sex shops.

■ There are strict criteria. Below is a list of content which is *not* permitted:
- any material which is in breach of criminal law
- material (including dialogue) likely to encourage an interest in abusive sexual activity (e.g. paedophilia)
- the portrayal of any sexual activity in which there is a lack of consent
- the infliction of pain or physical harm, real or simulated
- any sexual threats or humiliation which do not form part of clearly consenting role-play
- the use of any restraints which stop any individual from withdrawing their consent
- penetration by any object which is likely to cause physical harm
- activities which are degrading or dehumanising (e.g. bestiality, necrophilia, defecation)

■ The following content *is* permitted:
- aroused genitalia
- masturbation
- oral–genital contact, including kissing and licking
- penetration by fingers, penises, tongues, vibrators or dildos
- non-harmful fetish material
- group sexual activity
- ejaculation and semen

remake: a film which has the same title and storyline as a previous film and follows the original closely.

■ *e.g.* Gus Van Sant recreated Hitchcock's 1960 classic, *Psycho*, shot by shot in his 1998 version.

representation: the process by which a word, image or sound is invested with meaning and this meaning is communicated to the mind or imagination of the viewer.

■ Film-makers manipulate words, images and sounds to stand for larger ideas or *ideologies* (commonly associated with social groups, politics or sexuality, for example). Debates arise about positive and negative representations, though to some extent this comes down to subjective views. Discussions also arise when representation explores or exploits a *stereotype*.

retrospective: a series of films from a past period of film-making history, all in a particular style, from a particular *director* or featuring a particular *actor*.

■ A retrospective is usually shown in order to celebrate the life and work of a particular director or actor, or the films within a particular film movement.

■ *e.g.* the 2003 television retrospective of films featuring the recently deceased Katherine Hepburn

road movie: a film in which the central characters go on a journey, usually by car.

■ During the course of the journey the main characters will normally have a series of significant encounters, drive through a variety of landscapes, face challenges and eventually learn something about themselves and their experiences.

■ *e.g.* The *genre* 'road movie' includes a variety of *subgenres*, all utilising the structure of a road journey and illustrating a parallel inner journey on the part of the main character(s). *Ridley Scott*'s 1991 film *Thelma and Louise* is an often-quoted example of a female road movie, *Kalifornia* (Dominic Sena, 1993) features a main character who is a serial killer and Stephan Elliott's 1994 film *The Adventures of Priscilla, Queen of the Desert* tells the story of a group of transvestites. The recent British release, Ayub Khan-Din's *Heartlands*, is a serio-comic take on the road movie in which the journey is undertaken on a 50cc motorbike.

rockumentary: a film which uses the experiences of a rock band as its subject matter and follows real events which occur in the artists' lives.

■ *e.g.* Rob Reiner's spoof 1984 'rockumentary', *This Is Spinal Tap*

romantic comedy: a style of film in which the two main characters (usually very different from each other in terms of attitudes, wealth or social status) begin at odds with each other and end up becoming romantically involved.

■ Romantic comedies use the narrative strategy of a seemingly impossible match to illustrate the power of love or sexual attraction. The *conventions* of the *genre* create an expectation in the audience that the initial conflict or obstacles between the main characters will be overcome and a happy ending will ensue.

■ *e.g.* William Wyler's *Roman Holiday* (1953), Sharon Maguire's *Bridget Jones's Diary* (2000)

rough cut: an edited version of a film which lasts the same amount of time as the final version, but has not been fully edited.

■ A rough cut is important for the *director*, *cinematographer* and film *producer* as it shows them the whole film, rather than the small sections which they have seen up to this point. Further decisions concerning *editing* can be made after the rough cut has been analysed.

scene: a section of a film in which events occur in a particular place and time.

science fiction film: a style of film in which events occur in a futuristic or other-world setting.

■ Science fiction films often describe a situation in which scientific discovery has progressed much further than in the present. The setting for a science fiction film may be another world or space, or else, a future period on earth. Science fiction films are often based around a fear of what might happen in the future when technology has taken over or after a cataclysmic event has occurred (such as nuclear war). Science fiction films often use scenarios which mirror a fear existing in society or a contemporary social issue.

■ *e.g.* Fritz Lang's 1926 classic *Metropolis* describes a world where the ruling classes live in a paradisal setting, but the workers are treated as drones. American science fiction films of the 1950s, such as *It Came from Outer Space* (Jack Arnold, 1953), use alien invasion as an allegory for Communist takeover. Concerns about the abuse of scientific capability and the connected potential for science to get out of hand are explored in the two *Terminator* films (*James Cameron*, 1984 and 1991).

scopophilia: a term used by Sigmund Freud in his psychoanalytical writing which literally means 'a pleasure in looking'.

■ The term was later used by the *feminist* critic Laura Mulvey in her 1975 essay, 'Visual pleasure and narrative cinema', to describe the dominance of the male viewpoint in *mainstream* cinema. Mulvey's essay contended that the use of camera, characterisation and narrative within most mainstream films positioned the female characters as the object of the male gaze.

■ *e.g.* The films of director Alfred Hitchcock, which often include a female character who is manipulated, pursued or spied on by the male character, are cited by Mulvey as having a scopophilic focus. Marion Crane in *Psycho* (1960), for example, is watched through a peep hole by Norman Bates before she is murdered.

S

Scorsese, Martin (1942–): film *director*.

■ Born in New York, Scorsese studied film at the New York Film School before becoming one of the most famous directors of his generation. He commands much respect, from both critics and his peers. His films often articulate key periods in American history, but are equally well regarded as stylistically original discussions of the themes and human psychological states which exist in the contemporary world.

■ Filmography: *Who's That Knocking on My Door?* (1969), *Street Scenes* (1970), *Boxcar Bertha* (1972), *Mean Streets* (1973), *Alice Doesn't Live Here Anymore* (1974), *Italianamerican* (1974), *Taxi Driver* (1975), *New York, New York* (1977), *Raging Bull* (1980), *The King of Comedy* (1982), *After Hours* (1985), *The Color of Money* (1986), *The Last Temptation of Christ* (1988), *Goodfellas* (1990), *Cape Fear* (1991), *The Age of Innocence* (1993), *Casino* (1995), *Kundun* (1997), *Bringing Out the Dead* (1999), *Gangs of New York* (2002)

Scott, Ridley (1937–): film director.

■ Born in South Shields, Scott began his career as a set designer for the BBC and progressed to directing episodes of 1960s television series, such as *Z-Cars*. He then moved into the directing of commercials. The critical acclaim he received for this enabled him to move into film directing in the late 1970s.

■ Filmography: *The Duellists* (1977), *Alien* (1979), *Bladerunner* (1982), *Legend* (1985), *Someone to Watch Over Me* (1987), *Black Rain* (1989), *Thelma and Louise* (1991), *1492* (1992), *G.I. Jane* (1997), *Gladiator* (2000), *Black Hawk Down* (2002), *Matchstick Men* (2003)

screenplay: the written details of a film's dialogue, camerawork, lighting and settings which are used by the authors and director during the filming process. See also *shooting script*.

screen test: an audition in front of cameras which an actor has to have in order to get a part in a film.

screen writer: the person (or group of people) who writes the screenplay for a film.

screwball comedy: a type of *romantic comedy* in which one of the main protagonists is a sensible professional and the other has a more zany personality.

■ The more sensible character will be drawn into comic situations by the other character's quirkier and more liberated view of the world.

■ *e.g.* *Bringing up Baby* (Howard Hawks, 1938), in which the eccentric character played by Katherine Hepburn draws the more staid one played by Cary Grant into some very odd scenarios.

semiotics: the study of objects, sounds and images, and their potential meanings.

S

- The term was originally used by the Swiss linguist Ferdinand de Saussure (1857–1913). Semiotics studies the way in which an object, sound or image (called a 'sign' in semiotic theory) might have a literal and/or a suggested meaning. *Denotation* is the term in semiotics used to describe the literal meaning of a sign and *connotation* is the term used to describe the sign's suggested meanings.
- *e.g.* The sign '+' on a literal or denotation level is a cross. In some contexts its suggested meaning or connotation might be a plus sign, while for some people it might connote the Red Cross organisation.

sequel: a film which follows on from a previous one, taking up the story (and usually the continuing adventures of the same characters) after the earlier one left off. See also *prequel*.

- A successful film will often have at least one sequel, as it is deemed by the producers to be a safe financial bet.
- *e.g.* the *Alien* movies (*Aliens*, **James Cameron**, 1986, *Alien 3*, David Fincher, 1992, *Alien Resurrection*, Jean-Pierre Jeunet, 1997), *Mission Impossible II* (**John Woo**, 2000), *X-Men II* (Bryan Singer, 2003)

set: the artificially constructed environment in which a film is shot.

- A set is different from a *location*, as a set is created solely for the purposes of shooting a scene in a film whereas a location is a real place which is selected and chosen for filming.

setting: the place in which the story or parts of the story take place.

- Film settings have a considerable influence on viewers' interpretations and responses. They can mirror characters' emotions, establish place and time, evoke mood and atmosphere, and offer information about themes within a film.
- *e.g.* The snowbound, bleak landscape of the **Coen Brothers**' film *Fargo* (1996) sets up audience expectations about the characters and events. From the opening shots, which are almost completely filled with snow, we have a sense of a place which is isolated and isolating. The monotony of the snowy landscape and its monochrome palette act as a counterpoint to the dramatic and violent events which unfold in the film. In Sam Mendes's *American Beauty* (1999), meanwhile, the white picket fences, immaculate lawns and comfortable houses provide a picture-postcard surface covering up deep-seated frustrations and dissatisfactions in the characters' lives.

sexploitation film: a film which aims to titillate or sexually excite the viewer.

- These films are examples of soft-core *pornography* and generally receive a cinema release. The scenarios generally revolve around sexual interactions, rather than being driven by any well-developed plot.

S

■ *e.g.* Russ Meyer's films, such as *Faster, Pussycat! Kill! Kill!* (1966) and *Vixen* (1968) which show big-breasted women in various sexual scenarios

shooting script: the written information for a film, which includes dialogue, action, camera and lighting information, used by the cast and crew during filming. See also *screenplay*.

shot–reverse shot: the main type of camera shot used to film conversations.
■ A shot is taken over the shoulder of one of the characters to show the other character speaking. The next shot is of the same type but the other way round. These shots are then edited together and used in a conversation sequence to provide a break from shots showing the two characters together (*two-shots*).

silent film: early film without a soundtrack.
■ In the early days of film-making, many *Hollywood* stars either began their careers in silent film or spent their entire careers doing silent movies. Silent films are often characterised by over-the-top facial expressions and body language, used to convey meaning to the viewer.
■ *e.g.* *The Immigrant* and *Easy Street* (both 1917), starring Charlie Chaplin, D.W. Griffith's epic film *The Birth of a Nation* (1915)
■ *TIP* The first spoken words in film were in 1926 in Al Jolson's film *The Jazz Singer*.

slapstick comedy: a type of film which relies on physical humour and sight gags.
■ Slapstick comedies were particularly popular during the era of *silent film*, because they did not need dialogue in order to be funny.
■ *e.g.* the Keystone Kops comedies from the 1920s

slasher movie: a type of *horror film*.
■ Slasher films have certain ingredients which make them recognisable to a cinema audience. They frequently include a set of characters (often teenagers) who are 'picked off' one by one by an unknown killer, who is eventually confronted and killed by the 'final girl' left in a group. The 'slasher' label refers to the murder weapon which is some kind of knife or blade.
■ *e.g.* John Carpenter's *Halloween* (1978) is often cited as one of the first slasher films, although some critics consider Hitchcock's *Psycho* (1960) as the prototype. Subsequent examples of slasher films include *Friday 13th* (Sean Cunningham, 1980) and Wes Craven's *A Nightmare on Elm Street* (1984) and *Scream* (1996).

sleeper: a film which might not initially make money, but which eventually becomes a *box-office* success.

slow motion: the process by which the action in a film is slowed down.
■ Slow-motion sequences are sometimes used to increase tension in suspense or scary scenes, or to heighten the effect of an emotional moment.

social realism: the serious representation and discussion of particular social or political issues.

■ Social realist films use true-to-life characters and settings and may be shot in a naturalistic way (i.e. without the use of softening lighting or lenses).

■ *e.g.* many of the films of director Ken Loach, such as *Cathy Come Home* (1966) and *Kes* (1969)

soft focus: the effect gained when a special *lens* is attached to a *camera* which makes the subject of the shot appear to be framed by soft, hazy light.

■ Soft focus is usually associated with romance. A character as seen through the eyes of an admirer might be filmed in soft focus.

sound: the elements in a film which can be heard, rather than seen. See also *character theme, contrapuntal sound, non-diegetic sound, sound bridge, sound effects, sound track.*

sound bridge: sound which is sustained from one scene into the next.

■ A sound bridge extends a piece of music on the sound track or a sound from the story world over an edit. A sound may begin within one scene and continue into the next.

■ *e.g.* A director may decide to continue a piece of music associated with a character into a scene in which that character does not appear, thus indicating that the presence of the character is felt even in his/her absence.

■ *TIP* Being able to recognise the importance of elements such as sound bridges in the generation of meaning within a film text shows an understanding of the less obvious elements.

sound effect: sound which is added to a film in the *postproduction* stage to increase the impact and potential meaning of particular moments in a film.

■ *e.g.* During the making of the 1960s classic *Bonnie and Clyde,* the director Arthur Penn got the sound engineer to shoot bullets into a metal drum. The resulting rat-a-tat gunshot was inserted on the sound track for the film's shoot-out sequences.

sound track: a recording of all the sounds added to a film in *postproduction*.

■ These sounds are not heard by the characters within a film, but solely by the audience. Sound tracks are an essential part of the generation of meaning within a film. Music can convey much about character, settings, genre and atmosphere, while *voice-overs* can offer the viewer information to which characters within the film are not privy.

■ *e.g.* Bernard Herrmann's sound track for *Martin Scorsese*'s film *Taxi Driver* (1976) evokes a New York of loneliness and alienation. Vangelis's sound track for *Ridley Scott*'s film *Blade Runner* (1982) uses extended notes and industrial sounds in order to signal a futuristic and commerce-dominated environment.

S

spaghetti western: a type of *Western* which originally got its name because it was shot in Italy.

▨ Italy was used because it was cheaper than the American West and because it was Sergio Leone's country of origin.

▨ *e.g.* the films of Sergio Leone, such as *A Fistful of Dollars* (1964), *For a Few Dollars More* (1965) and *The Good, the Bad and the Ugly* (1966). All of these films starred Clint Eastwood.

special effects: the artificial elements of a film which are not real or do not really happen.

▨ Special effects include *computer-generated images*, *pyrotechnics* and artificial environments. Special effects are often associated with *science fiction* and *fantasy films*, but can also be used in genres such as *action films*, which require huge action sequences.

▨ *e.g.* Many shots of the ship in *James Cameron*'s *Titanic* (1997) were generated using computer technology. In an earlier era, much of the land of Oz in the film *The Wizard of Oz* (1939) was created by painting the settings onto a glass screen and then combining the shots of the characters and action with the glass screen background.

Spielberg, Steven (1946–): film *director*.

▨ Born in Cincinnati, USA, Spielberg is probably *the* most famous director working today. He began as a television director before entering film. He has been behind many of the biggest-grossing films of all time and his globally successful 1975 film *Jaws* is often cited as the first *blockbuster*. For years Spielberg was bypassed for the Best Director *Oscar*, but finally received it in 1993 for *Schindler's List*.

▨ Filmography: *The Sugerland Express* (1974), *Jaws* (1975), *Close Encounters of the Third Kind* (1977), *Raiders of the Lost Ark* (1981), *ET* (1982), *Indiana Jones and the Temple of Doom* (1984), *The Color Purple* (1985), *Empire of the Sun* (1987), *Indiana Jones and the Last Crusade* (1989), *Always* (1989), *Hook* (1991), *Jurassic Park* (1993), *Schindler's List* (1993), *The Lost World: Jurassic Park* (1997), *Amistad* (1997), *Saving Private Ryan* (1998), *AI* (2001), *Minority Report* (2002)

split screen: the effect of splitting the cinema screen in two, so as to allow two sets of events (normally occurring at the same time but in different locations) to be shown simultaneously.

▨ *e.g.* *Sliding Doors* (Peter Howitt, 1998)

stand-in: a person who takes the place of the actor during the setting up of lights and cameras.

▨ Stand-ins are chosen for their physical similarity to an actor, as their height and weight will affect the set-ups for the lighting and cameras.

star/star system: terms which refer, respectively, to the actors whose presence within a film usually secures a *box-office* success and the processes through which stars are created.

■ During the *golden age* of the *Hollywood studio system* (1930–48) stars were owned by particular studios for the 7 years of a particular contract. They made films only for that studio, starred in the films the studio chose for them, and had to allow their image to be fashioned by the studio to project a certain type of presence. Stars emerged out of studio 'stables' where they were 'groomed' and taught to walk, speak and live in a manner defined by the studio. Clark Gable, Gary Cooper, Humphrey Bogart and Jane Mansfield were all stars whose image was created in this way. Although stars within this system were guaranteed to make a certain number of films a year, they were not always satisfied with the role of studio product. The artistic freedom which today's stars enjoy was not possible and many stars were unhappy with being placed in a series of similar roles which would ultimately typecast them.

■ Stars today may find their niche within a particular *genre* or role and be expected by the industry and the audience to deliver what they are best associated with (in some cases to the point of typecasting), but they are not under the same contractual pressure as their predecessors and do have more control, not only over the films they choose, but often over content and direction. Because their presence in a film is so potentially lucrative for the producer, they can often influence production choices.

■ *e.g.* Tom Cruise has never won an Academy Award, but he is highly 'bankable': his box-office success secures him star status.

Steadicam: a portable camera held within a harness which can be strapped to a cameraman, so reducing the wobble of a *hand-held camera*.

■ The Steadicam enables the camera operator to move around without being affected by every change in the terrain of the set.

■ *e.g.* John Carpenter used the Steadicam during the opening sequence of *Halloween* (1978) in order to create the illusion that Michael Myers, whose point of view the audience is given, is walking up to and through his house in order to kill his sister.

stereotype: an oversimplified *representation* of a character.

■ A stereotyped character is not fully drawn and merely represents a set of characteristics, such as physical strength, moral courage or lecherousness, which the viewer expects from the role.

■ *e.g.* Many of the female characters in the *Hammer* horror films in the 1960s and 1970s were little more than screaming, whimpering victims, who only existed in the story in order to be killed by the 'monster' or rescued by the hero.

S

Stone, Oliver (1946–): film *director*.

■ Born in New York, Stone served in the US army during the Vietnam War and used this experience when creating his Vietnam films *Platoon* (1986) and *Born on the Fourth of July* (1989). Stone's most controversial film was *Natural Born Killers* (1994), which caused a moral panic and much debate concerning the effect of representations of violence on the cinema audience.

■ Filmography: *Seizure* (1974), *The Hand* (1981), *Salvador* (1985), *Platoon* (1986), *Wall Street* (1987), *Talk Radio* (1988), *Born on the Fourth of July* (1989), *The Doors* (1990), *JFK* (1991), *Heaven and Earth* (1993), *Natural Born Killers* (1994), *Nixon* (1995), *U-Turn* (1997), *Any Given Sunday* (1999)

stop-motion animation: *animation* which is created by the filming of fractional movements of models. When all the still images are edited together, there is an appearance of movement.

■ Stop-motion processes are time consuming and painstaking, but at one time they were the only way of offering a three-dimensional alternative to two-dimensional *cartoons*.

■ *e.g.* the films of animator Ray Harryhausen, such as *Jason and the Argonauts* (1963) and *Clash of the Titans* (1981)

■ *TIP* Although *computer-generated imagery* (CGI) is now the most common process for animated film production, stop motion has not become obsolete. Nick Park's Wallace and Grommit films (*The Wrong Trousers*, 1993 and *A Close Shave*, 1995) and *Chicken Run* (2000) are award-winning contemporary examples.

storyboard: a series of images with instructions to show how a *scene* will look when it is eventually filmed.

■ The storyboard provides an essential part of the initial planning for a film and is used by the *director* and *cinematographer* as a guideline for the shots needed in a scene.

straight-to-video: either a film which can never get cinema release or one which the producers fear will lose money at the box office.

■ Because of their explicit content, hard-core *pornographic* films are never given cinema release and are always straight-to-video.

studio: describes a company which is responsible for film *production*.

■ The term is most commonly used to describe companies responsible for film-making in Hollywood, but studios have existed and do exist in other countries (such as Britain's Ealing Studios in the 1930s, 1940s and 1950s). See also *golden age of Hollywood, Hollywood* and *studio system*.

studio system: a term used to describe the process of film production during the *Hollywood golden age* (1930–48).

▓ Five companies dominated the film industry at this time: Paramount, Loew's (the parent company of MGM), Fox Film, Warner Bros and RKO. Three other, smaller companies existed in Hollywood — Columbia, Universal and United Artists — but these did not own cinemas and needed to maintain a good relationship with the 'Big Five' in order to be sure of wide cinematic release. Paramount had more than 1,000 theatres in its cinema chain and as such had the biggest hold over film *exhibition*. Fox became Twentieth Century Fox in 1935 and from then on found financial success. RKO was the shortest-lived of the studios and the least profitable, despite producing films such as *Citizen Kane* (1941). MGM was perhaps the most famous of the major studios.

▓ All of the 'Big Five' were organised on a model of *vertical integration*. They each owned the means to produce, distribute and exhibit their films, and because of this they did not have to buy in the services of distributors or cinema owners and could keep all of their profits under one roof.

subgenre: a group of films which share the main characteristics of a larger group (or *genre*), but which use those characteristics in a slightly different way.

▓ *e.g.* Within the category of *horror films*, there exist the subgenres of demonic possession films, *slasher movies* and *vampire movies*. Comedies can be *romantic*, *screwball* and *slapstick*.

subjective camera: a camera shot or film style that provides the audience with a specific *point of view*.

▓ In this approach, the film-maker places the viewer in the position of a particular character.

subtitles: words on the screen which tell the audience what is being said in the dialogue.

▓ Subtitles are used to translate dialogue from a foreign language into the language spoken in the country where the film is being shown.

Sundance Film Festival: an independent film festival which takes place in Utah, USA.

▓ Sundance is also an organisation which aims to help young film-makers and promotes *independent* film. The organisation and the festival came about through the efforts of the actor Robert Redford.

superimposition: the placing of one image over another in a way that allows both images to be visible.

▓ A *dissolve* edit moves from one image to another by merging one image in and one image out. At a certain point within a dissolve the two images are seen on the screen at the same time and are thus superimposed.

Surrealism: a movement of writers, artists and film-makers. Surrealist films have dreamlike narratives and experimental camerawork.

S

■ In 1924 André Breton wrote a manifesto which outlined the importance of the unconscious in art. Directors such as Luis Buñuel and Jean Cocteau then translated Breton's manifesto into the creation of films which rejected usual patterns of time and presented images which seemingly emerged from the subconscious of the characters.

■ *e.g.* Buñuel's 1928 surrealist classic, *Un Chien Andalou*

surround sound: a technology which creates the impression that the sound elements of a film are coming from all parts of the cinema and not just the screen.

■ Surround-sound systems attempt to make audiences feel as if they are part of the action taking place on the cinema screen by placing them in the middle of the sound produced. This effect is achieved by the use of digital-quality sound.

suspense: a strategy used in film to create tension for the audience.

■ Suspense is generated when answers to questions are held back until the end of a film or when the viewer does not know what the outcome of an individual event will be. For the audience, suspense is an essential part of the pleasure of viewing films, especially *thrillers*, sometimes to the extent of generating a physical sensation of excitement.

■ *e.g.* Alfred Hitchcock created many films in which suspense was an essential factor. For instance, the reasons why Marnie (in the 1956 film of the same name) is in such a disturbed psychological state are held back until the end. Hitchcock once described the perfect suspense scenario as one in which a package with a bomb in it is being carried on a bus. The audience is forced to spend the whole of the bus journey fearing that the bomb might go off.

suture: a term used in audience response theory to describe the viewer being 'sewn into' a particular viewing position.

■ The suturing of an audience is achieved by a number of cinematic devices, such as camerawork and editing. If viewers are only shown events from a particular character's *point of view*, they are not able to see other events which may be significant. The audience is thus sutured into a particular viewpoint.

synergy: the release of two products, such as a film and a track from the film's sound track, at the same time, thus allowing for mutual advertising. The two products will have been produced by the same parent company.

■ Synergy allows producers to gain maximum exposure for a film release. Potential viewers may become interested through trailers and press information, but can also be made aware of a film through associated products.

■ *e.g.* The release of Baz Luhrmann's film *Moulin Rouge* (2001) was accompanied by the release of the track 'Moulin Rouge', sung by Christina Aguilera, Pink, Maya and Lil Kim.

synopsis: a brief description (usually about 200 words) of the main characters and events in a film.

■ A synopsis is often sent to journalists as part of a *press kit* intended to promote a forthcoming release.

take: a single run of film as it records a shot.

■ A *director* usually has a number of takes for each *scene* and then chooses the best or most appropriate during the *editing* stage.

Tarantino, Quentin (1963–): film *director*.

■ Born in Tennessee, USA, Tarantino famously worked in a video rental store before becoming a film director, which possibly accounts for his exhaustive knowledge of film. He is renowned for a style of film-making which uses fragmented narrative structures and time sequences, references to other films and periods from American popular culture and amoral but stylish characters.

■ Filmography: *Reservoir Dogs* (1991), *Pulp Fiction* (1994), *Jackie Brown* (1997)

teaser trailer: a brief section of a film shown as part of the *marketing* strategy for a forthcoming release.

■ Teaser trailers are shown to audiences before the release of the main trailer, in order to generate interest and word-of-mouth publicity. Teaser trailers only give hints concerning the look and content of a film in order to raise questions and whet appetites. Not all films have teaser trailers as well as the main trailer. They are usually associated with *blockbuster* films, which have the level of budget to allow for this kind of marketing.

Technicolor: a process developed at the beginning of the twentieth century for the production of colour film.

■ Films shot in Technicolor tend to have heightened or dazzling levels of colour.

■ *e.g.* *The Wizard of Oz* (1939) was the first film to use both black and white and Technicolor film.

teen movie: a film which is aimed specifically at a teenage market.

■ Teen movies feature characters, images and issues which are relevant to teenagers and reflect their own experiences.

■ *e.g.* The 1980s saw the release of many teen movies, including *The Breakfast Club* (John Hughes, 1985) and *Pretty in Pink* (Howard Deutch, 1986). *Clueless*

(1995), Amy Heckerling's modern adaptation of Jane Austen's novel *Emma* (1816), provides an example of a teen movie from the 1990s.

Third/Third World Cinema: refers to *Black Cinema* besides that which is produced within an African-American context.

■ Films identified as examples of Third or Third World Cinema are produced outside developed or Westernised countries. They share a thematic concern with colonisation, oppression and poverty.

■ *e.g.* Argentinian films such as *La Hora de los Hornos* (The Hour of the Furnaces, 1968) and *Piel de Verano* (Summer Skin, 1961) share the theme of political oppression.

35 mm: the standard film size, which is used for most professional filming.

■ 35 mm was introduced in 1889. For 70 mm film applications, see *big-screen cinema* and *IMAX*.

thriller: a *genre* of film in which the images and events presented aim to excite or disturb an audience.

■ Thrillers share a set of *conventions* which include an intricate plot, an anti-hero who draws the hero into this plot, a hero who has a flaw which affects his/her ability to challenge the anti-hero and a central crime. Thrillers differ from horror films in that they do not contain graphic scenes of violence or horrific events but create fear by more subtle means. Thrillers hold the audience's attention through *suspense* and by presenting a fallible hero in a perilous situation, struggling to provide resolution and *closure*.

■ *e.g.* Hitchcock's *Rear Window* (1954), *Kathryn Bigelow's Blue Steel* (1989), *David Fincher's Se7en* (1995)

tie-in: a product produced in connection with a film. See also *merchandising*.

■ Tie-ins can generate an enormous amount of money for the producers behind a film and are increasingly diverse in kind.

■ *e.g.* video and computer games, clothes, CDs, toys and games

tilt: a camera movement in which the base remains stationary, but the head of the camera moves vertically up or down.

■ Tilts are commonly used in order to position the viewer as a character within the film, looking up and down a building or sizing up another character.

top lighting: a type of light which comes from above.

■ Top lighting is often used to highlight the features of a character and make him/her appear more glamorous.

tracking shot: a camera movement where the camera follows the action on rails or tracks.

t

■ Tracking shots are often used to follow action, such as a moving train, or to take the viewer on a journey through different parts of a scene.

■ *e.g.* Robert Altman's film *The Player* (1992), which concerns the film industry, opens with a long tracking shot showing different parts of a studio complex.

trailer: a series of short extracts edited together to create an advert for a forthcoming film.

■ In order to sell a film to prospective audiences, a trailer aims to exhibit a number of features: *genre*, key elements of the story and characters. If the film is a *star* vehicle, scenes may be chosen to highlight the star's role. If the unique selling point (USP) of the film is the *director*, the voice-over will highlight this and may refer to previous films by that director.

■ *e.g.* Trailers for the *Harry Potter* films withhold much of the story information but contain a series of short, dynamic sequences from the more dramatic scenes.

■ *TIP* Trailers can have different certificates from the films themselves. If a trailer for a 15-certificate film is shown to an audience that includes younger children, the trailer has to be compatible with a 12 or PG certificate.

12A cinema/12 video: levels of film classification. In the 12A cinema category, no child under 12 may see the film unless accompanied by an adult. In the 12 video category, no child younger than 12 can buy or rent the video.

■ The criteria which the *British Board of Film Classification* uses in order to assess films for a 12A or 12 rating are:
- Mature themes (such as racism) are acceptable, but they should be treated in a way which is suitable for a young teenager.
- The use of strong language must be rare and entirely suitable to context.
- Nudity is allowed, but if it is in a sexual context, it must be very brief.
- Sexual activity may be implied; sexual references should be appropriate to the sex education knowledge of young teenagers.
- Violence should not be detailed and there should be no emphasis on blood or injuries. Sexual violence can be implied, but no physical detail should be given.
- Techniques which can be imitated, such as fighting, should not be made realistic or easy to copy.
- Horror strategies such as a sustained sense of menace are allowed.
- References to drugs and brief images of soft drugs (e.g. cannabis) are allowed, although anything which appears glamorising or instructive is not.

Twentieth Century Fox: a major *Hollywood* studio, created in 1935 by the merger of Fox Film Corporation and Twentieth Century Pictures and still in existence today.

■ Twentieth Century Fox was a powerful force in the *studio system* during the *golden age of Hollywood* (1930–48).

two-shot: a shot with two people in the same frame.

■ Two-shots are commonly used to show a conversation taking place between two characters. Both characters can be seen in a shot of this kind. See also *shot–reverse shot*.

U: a level of film classification which indicates films suitable for audiences aged 4 years and over.

■ Films with a U certificate have to fulfil certain criteria:
- The treatment of problematic themes must be sensitive and appropriate to a younger audience.
- Bad language may only be very mild and infrequent.
- Occasional natural nudity is allowed, but with no sexual context.
- Only mild sexual behaviour (e.g. kissing) and references (e.g. to 'making love') are permitted.
- Any violence must be very mild.
- There can be no emphasis on weapons which might appear realistic.
- If any horror effects are involved, these should be very mild and should have a reassuring outcome.
- No references may be made to drugs or drug use.

Uc: a level of film classification which indicates that films are especially suitable for pre-school children.

Underground Cinema: a term used to describe films which reject the structure, look and content of *mainstream cinema.*

■ Underground films often use a more experimental style and contentious subject matter. They may be concerned with radical political ideas, anti-establishment ideas, taboos and other subjects which would not be popular with mainstream cinema audiences.

■ *e.g.* the films produced in the 1960s by directors such as Andy Warhol

underlighting: a lighting effect where the main source of light in a scene comes from below.

■ Underlighting often has a distorting effect and can be used to make an object or character seem threatening.

■ *e.g. Horror films* often use underlighting in order to make the audience feel scared of a character or fearful of an object.

unit: describes a particular group of individuals who deal with one aspect of the shooting of a film.

■ Any one film will have a *camera* unit, a *lighting* unit and a *sound* unit.

United Artists: a film company which was begun in 1919 by the actors Charlie Chaplin, Mary Pickford and Douglas Fairbanks, and the director D. W. Griffith, in order to distribute their own films.

■ United Artists was created in an attempt to break away from the control of the big studios and give the actors concerned more creative influence over their own films. United Artists became part of *MGM* in 1981.

■ *e.g.* Some of the most famous examples of United Artists' films are *Stagecoach* (John Ford, 1940), *Rebecca* (Alfred Hitchcock, 1940) and *Night of the Hunter* (Charles Laughton, 1955).

Universal: a film production company created in 1921.

■ Universal was not as large as the 'Big Five' *Hollywood* studios and did not own cinema chains, so it needed to maintain good relations with the major studios in order to get its films screened. Universal was bought by the massive media conglomerate Vivendi in 2000.

■ *e.g.* Films produced by Universal include *All Quiet on the Western Front* (Lewis Milestone, 1930), *Dracula* (Tod Browning, 1931), *All that Heaven Allows* (Douglas Sirk, 1955), *Jaws* (*Steven Spielberg*, 1975), *The Deer Hunter* (Michael Cimino, 1978), *Jurassic Park* (Steven Spielberg, 1993) and *Gladiator* (*Ridley Scott*, 2000).

utopia: a future or alternative world in which everything is perfect.

■ Coined by Sir Thomas More (1478–1535) as the name of an imaginary island, and literally meaning 'no place' in Greek, the term refers to a land where the best possible form of government prevails and humans coexist peacefully.

■ *Science fiction* films may begin with an apparently utopic situation, only for the peace and safety to be shattered and a nightmarish *dystopia* to develop.

■ *e.g. Steven Spielberg*'s film *Minority Report* (2002) begins with images of a future world which is apparently safe and lawful. The problems underlying this untroubled surface are discovered by the character played by Tom Cruise, and the rest of the film deals with his attempts to find the truth behind the fiction.

vampire movie: a *horror film* which draws its characters and scenarios from tales of blood-sucking, undead creatures.

■ Vampire films have been successful throughout cinema history. They present fantasy horror scenarios in which the central character both seduces and kills his (mainly female) victims. Vampire films contain characteristic elements such as castles, coffins, wooden stakes, crucifixes, entranced victims, bats and heroes who eventually destroy the vampire. Bram Stoker's classic novel *Dracula* (1897) has provided the basis of many horror films.

■ *e.g.* the 1921 vampire classic *Nosferatu* (F. W. Murnau) and *Francis Ford Coppola*'s more recent vampire film *Bram Stoker's Dracula* (1991)

vertical integration: describes the ownership of all stages of film production, distribution and exhibition by one company.

■ During the *golden age* of the *Hollywood studio system*, the five major companies — Paramount, Loew's (the parent company of MGM), Fox Film, Warner Bros and RKO — each owned the means to produce, distribute and exhibit their films. This allowed them to dominate the film industry until in 1948 a Supreme Court ruling known as the 'Paramount Decree' forced them to sell their cinemas and thus broke up their model of vertical integration.

video games/related films: films which initially existed as video or computer games.

■ The film industry trades on the popularity of the gaming industry in various ways. If a certain game has a pre-existing consumer base, a film of that game may have a ready-made audience.

■ Video and computer games are also exploited as resource materials for new films, providing characters, scenarios, settings and even basic narratives.

■ Games can be lucrative avenues for *merchandising*. Spin-off games from films such as the *Harry Potter* series or the *Lord of the Rings* trilogy provide a huge potential for ancillary (extra) profits.

■ From the point of view of consumers, however, films which began life as

V

computer or video games may be less than satisfying. If the unique selling point (USP) of a game is its interactive potential, the viewer may be disappointed by the film, which by its nature offers a non-interactive experience.

■ *e.g. Tomb Raider* (Simon West, 2001), *Resident Evil* (Paul W. S. Anderson, 2002)

video nasties: coined in the 1980s by the press and politicians to describe films on video which were believed to include exceptionally gratuitous images of violence and to have a negative influence on those who watched them.

■ The video nasties debate was at its height in the early 1980s, due to the naming of certain videos in criminal trials. The killing of toddler James Bulger by two 10-year-old boys caused a moral panic focusing on the video *Child's Play III* (although it was never proved that the boys who killed James Bulger had seen it), which was eventually pulled from distribution.

■ The *Video Recordings Act 1984* was introduced in order to control what could be released on video. When the moral panic over video nasties subsided, many films which had previously been denied video certification were reassessed.

■ *e.g. Driller Killer, SS Extermination Camp* and *Cannibal Holocaust* were all originally available on video but were denied video certification after the 1984 Video Recordings Act.

Video Recordings Act 1984: government legislation which meant that films on video had to be certified for release by the *British Board of Film Classification*.

■ Films on video are treated slightly differently from films shown at the cinema, in terms of classification. When a film is shown in the home, it is much more difficult to control who is viewing it, so films are either given a higher certificate when transferred to video or heavily cut.

virtual reality: a technology which allows the creation or re-creation of a place or an event.

■ Virtual reality gives the individuals experiencing it the impression that they are taking part in real events or exist in a real setting.

■ *e.g.* The Wachowski Brothers' 1999 film *The Matrix* uses the idea of virtual realities. The character of Neo (played by Keanu Reeves) is trained in a virtual setting and has spent much of his life in a world which he later discovers has been created by a computer.

voice-over: a *commentary* or narration heard only by the audience.

■ As part of a documentary film, the voice-over explains and discusses the content. In a feature film, the voice-over has a similar function, but it is often a character from the story world who acts as the narrator.

■ *e.g.* Sam Mendes's film *American Beauty* (1999) opens with a voice-over from the central character, Lester, immediately making the audience aware that the events in the film will be filtered through Lester's consciousness.

V

■ *TIP* Remember that the voice-over within a feature film may be unreliable. The character who acts as your guide through the text will have a subjective response to the events he or she is commenting on, and may be influenced by bias, ulterior motives or a private agenda. Leonard Shelby, for example, the narrator in Christopher Nolan's film *Memento* (2000), cannot remember recent events and is therefore an unreliable narrator.

voyeurism: the act of watching somebody else without his/her knowledge or permission.

■ Voyeurism has been used as the basis for many films, but is also discussed within film theory as a factor in the pleasure the audience gets from watching a film. See also *scopophilia*.

■ *e.g.* The central character in Michael Powell's chilling 1960 film *Peeping Tom* is obsessed with watching and gains his pleasure from spying on his intended victims before killing them.

war film: a type of film in which the action takes place during a war.

■ War films usually draw their storylines from real historical conflicts and offer comment on the military decisions taken and the human consequences of these decisions.

■ *e.g.* Acclaimed First World War films include *All Quiet on the Western Front* (Lewis Milestone, 1930) and *Paths of Glory* (Stanley Kubrick, 1957). The Vietnam War provides the background for events in numerous films, including *Platoon* (**Oliver Stone**, 1986) and *Born on the Fourth of July* (Oliver Stone, 1989), both of which offer an image of the Vietnam War as brutal and confusing for the soldiers.

Warner Bros: a major *Hollywood* film company which was founded in 1923 by four brothers: Harry, Albert, Sam and Jack Warner.

■ Warner Bros was bought by Ted Turner's Time Inc. organisation in 1990 and then merged with Turner Broadcasting in 1996 to become TimeWarner. In 2000 this new company merged again, with AOL, to produce the massive media conglomerate AOL/TimeWarner.

■ *e.g.* Warner Bros produced some extremely famous films, including *Casablanca* (Michael Curtiz, 1942) and *Bonnie and Clyde* (Arthur Penn, 1967).

Western: a term used to describe a *genre* of films which are set in the Wild West of America.

■ Widely regarded as the archetypal American films, Westerns exploit a set of conventions, such as cowboys, Indians, ranches, saloons, gunfights and sheriffs. They also include certain pairs of oppositions within their thematic structure, such as civilisation versus the wild and good versus evil.

■ Westerns have evolved in recent years and now include examples of films in which the gunslinger is female or, if male, is old and unglamorous.

■ *e.g.* Classic Westerns are associated with directors such as John Ford and Sergio Leone. More recent examples include *The Unforgiven* (Clint Eastwood, 1992), in which Clint Eastwood plays an old, bitter gunfighter, and *The Quick and the*

Dead (Sam Raimi, 1995), in which Sharon Stone plays a female gunfighter set on revenge.

whip pan: a camera movement from left to right or right to left which is so quick as to disorientate the viewer.

■ Whip pans can be used to represent a character's *point of view* when he/she sees something too quickly to gain a clear view. They can also reveal fleeting glimpses of locations, leaving the viewers wondering what they actually saw.

wide (-angled) shot: a shot which incorporates 60 degrees of vision, rather than the usual 45–50 degrees.

■ A wide-angled shot might be used to generate a sense of the size and magnitude of a particular location.

widescreen: a cinema screen technology which presents images in a much wider than standard format. See *big screen cinema* and *IMAX*.

wipe: an edit type in which one image appears to wipe another off the screen.
■ Wipes are often used for transitions between different locations portrayed at the same time.

Woo, John (1946–): film *director*.
■ Born in Guangzhou, China, Woo moved to Hong Kong with his family while he was young and it was here that he achieved his first film successes. After transferring to Hollywood, Woo became famous for his action films which included huge, highly choreographed action scenes and pyrotechnical displays.
■ Filmography:
Cantonese *The Young Dragons* (1973), *The Dragon Tamers* (1974), *The Hand of Death* (1976), *Princess Chang Ping* (1976), *Follow the Star* (1977), *Money Crazy* (1978), *Last Hurrah for Chivalry* (1978), *Hello, Late Homecomers* (1978), *From Rags to Riches* (1979), *Laughing Times* (1981), *To Hell with the Devil* (1982), *Plain Jane to the Rescue* (1982), *Heroes Shed no Tears* (1983), *The Time You Need a Friend* (1984), *Run Tiger Run* (1985), *A Better Tomorrow* (1986), *A Better Tomorrow II* (1987), *The Killer* (1989), *Just Heroes* (1990), *A Bullet in the Head* (1990), *Hard Boiled* (1992)
English *Once a Thief* (1991), *Hard Target* (1993), *Broken Arrow* (1996), *Face/Off* (1997), *Mission Impossible II* (2000)

wrap: the end of a day's filming or of a whole shoot.

zombie film: a type of film in which the living dead are seen to be a malevolent force, seeking to kill (in some films by eating) the living.

■ Zombie films usually have simplistic narratives in which the dead either come or are brought back to life and spend the rest of the film attacking the living characters.

■ *e.g.* *The Night of the Living Dead,* filmed by a group of film-makers in Pittsburgh in 1968, proved to be hugely influential. One of its makers, George Romero, went on to make a career from the zombie genre.

zoom: a single shot which moves either towards a particular subject or away from it.

■ A variable focus or zoom *lens* allows for a (usually) rapid movement into or away from a particular subject. Both types of shot create the illusion of displacement in time and space and can be used to disorientate the viewer.

■ *e.g.* The end of the opening sequence in Wes Craven's *Scream* (1996) involves a jagged zoom into the dead body of the character Casey Becker. Her mother's horror is indicated by the brutal focus of this *point of view* zoom shot.

■ *TIP* Zooms are a means by which a director can manipulate the audience's focus and concentrate the viewers' gaze on something specific in the frame.